DONE
right

DONE
right

How Tomorrow's Top
Leaders Get Work Done

ALEX SHOOTMAN

Done Right: How Tomorrow's Top Leaders Get Stuff Done
Published by Rocket Surgery Publishing
Lehi, Utah

Library of Congress Control Number: 2018956315
SHOOTMAN, ALEX, Author
DONE RIGHT
ALEX SHOOTMAN

ISBN: 978-1-7326676-0-0

BUS071000   **BUSINESS & ECONOMICS** / Leadership
BUS041000   **BUSINESS & ECONOMICS** / Management

Cover Design by Ryan Braman

QUANTITY PURCHASES: Schools, companies, professional groups, clubs, and other organizations may qualify for special terms when ordering quantities of this title. For information, email Info@DoneRightBook.com.

ROCKET SURGERY
PUBLISHING

This book is dedicated to the over 3,000 customers of Workfront. So many of you have welcomed me into your workplace and shared your hopes and dreams for your company, your team, and yourself. I learned from you that work can be an essential part of human dignity. You inspire me, and you are why we do what we do at Workfront.

Table of Contents

Exercise Workflow

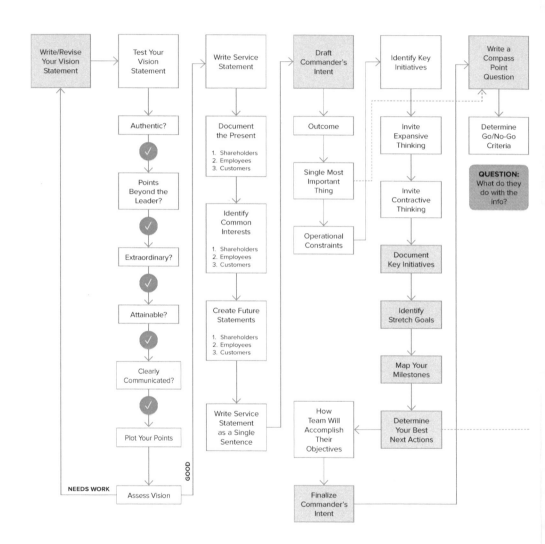

Write/Revise Your Vision Statement → **Test Your Vision Statement** → **Write Service Statement** → **Draft Commander's Intent** → **Identify Key Initiatives** → **Write a Compass Point Question**

Test Your Vision Statement
- Authentic? ✓
- Points Beyond the Leader? ✓
- Extraordinary? ✓
- Attainable? ✓
- Clearly Communicated? ✓
- Plot Your Points
- Assess Vision

NEEDS WORK / GOOD

Write Service Statement
- Document the Present
  1. Shareholders
  2. Employees
  3. Customers
- Identify Common Interests
  1. Shareholders
  2. Employees
  3. Customers
- Create Future Statements
  1. Shareholders
  2. Employees
  3. Customers
- Write Service Statement as a Single Sentence

Draft Commander's Intent
- Outcome
- Single Most Important Thing
- Operational Constraints
- How Team Will Accomplish Their Objectives
- Finalize Commander's Intent

Identify Key Initiatives
- Invite Expansive Thinking
- Invite Contractive Thinking
- Document Key Initiatives
- Identify Stretch Goals
- Map Your Milestones
- Determine Your Best Next Actions

Write a Compass Point Question
- Determine Go/No-Go Criteria

QUESTION: What do they do with the info?

PRE-PROJECT KICKOFF MEETING

TIMELINE

Download all the exercises at **donerightbook.com**

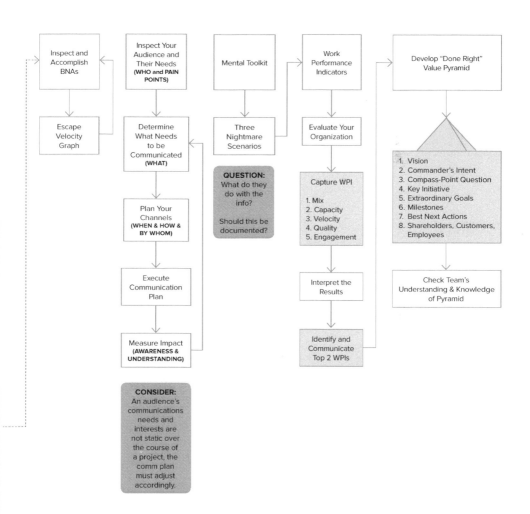

| Inspect and Accomplish BNAs | Inspect Your Audience and Their Needs (WHO and PAIN POINTS) | Mental Toolkit | Work Performance Indicators | Develop "Done Right" Value Pyramid |

Escape Velocity Graph

Determine What Needs to be Communicated (WHAT)

Three Nightmare Scenarios

Evaluate Your Organization

QUESTION:
What do they do with the info?

Should this be documented?

Plan Your Channels (WHEN & HOW & BY WHOM)

Capture WPI

1. Mix
2. Capacity
3. Velocity
4. Quality
5. Engagement

1. Vision
2. Commander's Intent
3. Compass-Point Question
4. Key Initiative
5. Extraordinary Goals
6. Milestones
7. Best Next Actions
8. Shareholders, Customers, Employees

Execute Communication Plan

Interpret the Results

Check Team's Understanding & Knowledge of Pyramid

Measure Impact (AWARENESS & UNDERSTANDING)

Identify and Communicate Top 2 WPIs

CONSIDER:
An audience's communications needs and interests are not static over the course of a project, the comm plan must adjust accordingly.

PROJECT EXECUTION AND MEASUREMENT

Attribution: Mike Kilbane | Principal at Stratsys Services

Foreword

BY RAY WANG, PRINCIPAL ANALYST, FOUNDER,
AND CHAIRMAN OF SILICON VALLEY
BASED CONSTELLATION RESEARCH, INC.

The modern workplace has radically transformed. Where we work, how we work, what we work on, who we work with, and why we work no longer appear the same. As five generations of workers enter the modern workforce, leaders face challenges in how they inspire their organizations to execute in highly competitive market places. Not only do leaders have to attract the right talent, but they also have to ensure that their teams can succeed in the right organizational structure while dealing with massive change. This shift requires some new modus operandi for culture, leadership, and vision. Organizations need a defining direction.

Getting to this point cannot be achieved through randomness or luck. A defined path requires a codification of culture and a methodology. Management gurus, for years, have come up with new approaches;

however, they have often overemphasized one element at the expense of a holistic model. Moreover, techniques have become stale. In highly dynamic markets, agility trumps continuity, engagement overcomes passivity, and data-driven decisions augment gut instinct.

This intense pursuit of success requires an appreciation of the organizational life cycle and starts with fundamental human elements, such as clearly defining a mission and purpose, understanding human psychology, developing non-monetary and monetary incentives, crafting a culture of discipline on attention, ensuring agility, and measuring work for the purposes of improvement.

While these fundamental changes may appear hard at first, getting work done and done right requires both a qualitative and quantitative aspect. The new world of work must balance each individual's innate left-brain and right-brain capabilities. These new digital artisans bring a goal-minded approach that transcends dysfunctional momentum and focuses the team on the mission and purpose.

These new paradigms of leadership help tomorrow's leaders get work done and done right. Bolstered by an orchestrated set of employee experiences, leadership guiding principles, and business agility, the future of work presents new opportunities. When done right, we can expect to master modern work and craft a meaningful future for all.

Preface

BY JORDAN STAPLES,
DIRECTOR OF TRAINING AT WORKFRONT

You are facing a digital crisis. The *digital transformation* we often reference today has democratized innovation, opening up opportunities for any business to deliver differentiating products and services to the market. However, digitization has obliterated your operating model, leaving your team crippled in the gray area between analog and digital work.

Sure, this new digital age has created new norms like speed and connectivity, but it has also exposed a new reality. Every day your team wrestles with clashing priorities and disjointed work streams across a disconnected company that is buried in exabytes of digital assets. The byproduct is a workforce of manual "digital" laborers who are afraid of not doing the right work at the right time. No team can be effective, let alone innovative, when they are working in this type of environment.

This is the digital work crisis you face today.

While executives, shareholders, and customers demand value, your team is starving to contribute to something greater than themselves. The onus falls on every leader to radically rethink how they empower their teams to execute and deliver value in the Digital Era.

Here at Workfront, we call this new wave of leadership *modern work management.*

Modern work management is about empowering your team to execute purpose-driven work at the speed and scale of digital. If you believe, like we do, that great work happens when your people finish strong and win together, then (as their leader), you have to orchestrate and automate what they are being asked to do. If you do, speed and scale will follow. This is the modern formula for delivering differentiated products and services to your market and customer base.

This book offers a practical guide to leading with purpose. You will learn to orchestrate the way your team and organization works from the experience of a lot of leaders just like yourself. The opportunity to elevate your business and career are here. So, my question to you is simple — what will you do about it?

Introduction

Masters of Modern Work

"Adapt or perish, now as ever,
is nature's inexorable imperative."

—H.G. WELLS

A little after 12:30 p.m. on Wednesday, May 2, 2018, I was sitting between two customers at the Solario Restaurant inside the Gaylord Opryland Resort in Nashville. We were all there for Workfront's annual LEAP Customer Conference, and I was enjoying listening to a customer towards the end of his career picking the brain of a young leader, Alison Angilletta, who is more formally introduced later in this book.

"Who is your executive sponsor?" the customer asked.

"Why, it's me," Alison replied. "I was responsible for some great results last year, got promoted to director, and now have people on my team doing the job that I was doing before."

The customer smiled, nodded, and offered his hearty congratulations.

I've been fortunate to be part of three different software companies that created brand new categories. In each situation, young, gifted leaders had the foresight to use these new categories as rocket fuel for their careers. When I've met with these leaders and we get past the topic of the technology we are discussing, they always steer the conversation to what they *really* value: learning how to get things done in modern, geographically distributed, dynamic, and competitive enterprises. They want to be the one in their company to succeed by mastering the change that is occurring.

Today I am at Workfront and leaders like Alison are using technology to help their companies take advantage of their greatest opportunities. These leaders want to have an impact, they want to pitch in and make a difference, and they're looking for practical ways to get things done. Essentially, they want to be masters of modern work. Their ambition is the inspiration for this book.

If you want to be a master of modern work, you'll find practical advice, tested techniques, and immediately usable exercises in every chapter, all of which reflect the combined, earned knowledge of more than thirty proven leaders from different industries and walks of life. I'll add to that some scars from my own mistakes and observations from my current vantage point at Workfront, where I see young leaders using our technology to show their companies how to get work done right.

Let me introduce the cast of leaders interviewed for this book. I've taken counsel from adventurers like Debra Searle, who rowed solo across the Atlantic and developed mindset techniques that can cope with any challenge. I've spoken with my friend Mark McGinnis, a US Navy SEAL commander with a distinguished record, who has served on operations around the world. I've talked to academics like Tony Crabbe and Eddie Obeng, who've studied — and advised — some of the world's biggest businesses and best-known brands. I've heard from futurists such as Alan Lepofsky and James Wallman, who see further and faster than most folks and are hired by major corporations to help them see around the corner. And I've tapped the insight of leaders in fields as diverse as healthcare, financial services, manufacturing and engineering, and multimedia entertainment. You'll learn from Sean Pederson how Trek Bicycles made one of their signature products. And you'll discover what lessons Cynthia Boon learned on her journey from 911 call dispatcher to the senior leadership at General Motors Financial. James Veall of Viacom — the company behind Nickelodeon, Paramount, and MTV — gives his thoughts on how demographics will reshape the future of work. And for advice on communication, you'll hear from three of the best-known marketers in the business — Jay Baer, Lee Odden, and Brian Carroll — who have told me what works in their own organizations.

There are many other brilliant commentators, including Dave Randall at Atlas Copco, Claudia Brozda at Dräger, Kathy Haven at FCB, Kevin Ellington at LeapPoint, Scott Shippy at Viasat, Amy Spencer at Blackbaud, Erica Gunn at a major fashion retailer, Eric Lucas at Crowley Maritime Corporation, Tom Amies-Cull at Dentsu Aegis Network, Jen Gilligan, formerly at the *Daily Telegraph* (currently an adventure-seeker), Vic Alejandro at Denver Water, and Philip Stickland at Adventist Health System. In addition, personal mentors and friends such as Art Wilson, George Biel, and Rob McKenna influenced my thinking over the years.

The result is a book that walks through the principles and practices that are the foundation of mastering modern work. I am convinced that in the modern enterprise the most important personal and sustainable competitive advantage anyone can have is the ability to get stuff done. So, think of this book like a trail map that shows you everything from the first steps you need to take to measuring your success when the job is done. Let's embark on our journey. It all starts with how you make work matter.

1

Make Work Matter

"No matter what anybody tells you,
words and ideas can change the world."

—ROBIN WILLIAMS, AS MR. KEATING IN *DEAD POET'S SOCIETY*

"We choose to go to the moon in this decade and do the other things, not because they are easy, but because they are hard," President John F. Kennedy said in the late summer of 1962.[1] History remembers the eloquence and high ideals of his moon-shot speech. Yet, what echoes through the decades is just a fragment of what the president told the assembled crowd at Rice University in Texas that day. For sure, he raised the nation's eyes to the heavens. And he acknowledged that America was trailing in the space race after cosmonaut Yuri Gagarin's first orbital flight a year before. But less famously, JFK broke down the grandeur of the endeavor in ways everyone could understand. The cost of a moon-shot? "Less than we pay for cigarettes and cigars every year," said the president. He also put the cost at no more than "fifty cents a week for every man, woman, and child in the United States."

No one listening doubted the technological ambition of the project. But after the speech they could also see, perhaps for the first time, that the vision was viable. They could get a human on the moon for just fifty cents a week.

You're unlikely to hear cosmic ambition in most boardrooms, offices, or on conference calls. But the leaders who are best able to persuade and motivate others turn grand visions into realities, just as JFK did. Great leaders persuade everyone embarking on a journey to believe they can reach the end, however uncomfortable the path ahead. Some develop this skill through experience; a few are born with a gift for visionary thinking and language. I believe everyone can and must learn how to make work matter.

Unfortunately, as Harvard professor Teresa Amabile shows, too many workers today are "quietly disengaged from what they do, and their performance is suffering as a result."[2] Such workers don't think they're making progress. This employee dissatisfaction leads to slower revenue growth and lower profitability compared to businesses where employees feel fully engaged. Amabile puts the cost to the US economy at a staggering $300 billion per year. That's more than half of the nation's annual investment in research and development.[3] As she says, "It doesn't have to be this way. Work should ennoble, not kill, the human spirit."

This chapter illustrates how you can do just that — ennoble the human spirit. We'll show why it's critical to start with outlook; then we'll outline how to master motivation and vision. From there we'll look at why pride matters more than money, and why meaningful work matters more than return on investment. Finally, we'll look at how mundane tasks can carry a clearer sense of purpose.

START WITH OUTLOOK

There are two worldviews in leadership. Some leaders believe people go to work with the intent to do their best. Other leaders take the view that people's prevailing instinct is to shirk. The first leadership outlook creates a culture of trust, collaboration, and innovation. The second creates a workplace where everyone looks over their shoulder and refuses to try new things for fear of failing.

Your leadership outlook will shape the climate and culture of your business. It will also help answer the questions that everyone cares about. As the author Jay Baer said in our interview, "Workers are always going to wonder why they're there, how they fit in, if they're being treated fairly, and how they can advance themselves. Those are really the only questions that matter."

It's the difference between action and *purposeful* action. When people don't believe they're valued or that there's value in their work, they dream of being somewhere else — frankly, anywhere else.

If you're absolutely convinced that people come to work with the intent to just get by, you might want to put this book down now. The next nine chapters will really frustrate you. I believe people are generally good and want to do great work — work that matters. And making work matter is too important to leave to chance. It's why if you want to be a master of modern work, you have to master motivation and vision.

MASTER MOTIVATION AND VISION

Motivation

If you lead any type of work, you're accountable to motivate others to do that work well. For any of us to have a chance at being extraordinarily motivated, to really be driven by passion, we have to be able to answer these three basic questions:

1. Do you know your role?
2. Do you believe your role matters?
3. Do you have a chance to be proud of your work?

If you and your team members aren't able to answer these questions well, you haven't yet created an environment where people see that their work matters. It is up to you, as the leader, to get these questions answered in such a way that people are intrinsically motivated. Much of this book is dedicated to helping you answer these three questions for the folks you lead.

Human nature dictates we thrive when we feel we're making the best of our unique attributes as part of a team. Motivation hinges on being proud of your team's collective work. Only then can you actually reach your goals.

To this end, reflect upon a time in which you could answer these three questions well. What were the conditions that existed? Did your team also know their role within the organization? Did you all play to your strengths? If you recall, it all started with everyone knowing where they were going. It all started with a shared and well-understood vision.

Vision

Vision gives everyone a clear and compelling answer to the question: *"Why am I working here?"* It's rooted in four elements. The vision:

1. Is focused on authenticity and hope.
2. Points beyond the leader.
3. Is extraordinary but attainable.
4. Is easily communicated.

What you see here is a healthy mix of optimism and pragmatism — and you need both. Let's compare two vision statements. First,

Hilton Hotel's long-held vision, which has been "to fill the earth with the light and warmth of hospitality." This vision is certainly hopeful, points beyond the leader, and is easy to articulate. But is it attainable? Scratch at the sentiment, and it's unclear if anyone would know when this vision has been achieved. That might not matter to those employees who seek an optimistic purpose, but it might not chime with more practically-minded employees. Now, look at Nick Swinmurn's founding vision for his company, Zappos. Swinmurn didn't want to save the world; he wanted to build an enduring clothing and shoe business online:

> One day, 30 percent of all retail transactions in the US will be online. People will buy from the company with the best service and the best selection. Zappos.com will be that online store.

Again, the vision was simply expressed, hopeful, and looked beyond the founder — indeed, Swinmurn left the business in 2006. As ecommerce accounts for only about 9 percent of transactions in the US, it was also an extraordinary future goal.[4] The Zappos vision was about prospering in a growing market — and spelled out the way that would happen. They would win by offering the best service and best selection. Everyone in the business could take a cue from the vision and apply it to their own work.

In a perfect world, you would create a vision that was somewhere between Hilton's ambition and Swinmurn's ground-level approach. There are dreamers and realists in every business, and you need a vision that speaks to both. Ask yourself one question: What keeps your best individuals and best teams in your business? Your answer will lead you to clearly articulate your vision, which will in turn inspire your team members to make work matter. Vision is not just for a company; it is also needed for anything that people spend time trying to accomplish.

PRIDE MATTERS MORE THAN MONEY

At this point you may have questions — maybe even a hint of doubt. Perhaps you're thinking, "These are fine words about motivation and vision, Alex, but surely people make choices about where they work based on what they're paid?"

McKinsey researcher Jon R. Katzenbach makes a compelling case that "pride matters more than money."[5] By studying organizations such as the US Marine Corps, Katzenbach shows that when people learn they're capable of much more than they thought possible, anticipatory pride becomes their driving motivational force. He traces pride as a motivating force back to childhood — that early instinct we have as children to make our parents or caregivers proud of our achievements. We want to see them glow when we win that race or come home with good grades on our report card. According to Katzenbach, that instinct endures but evolves as we move into our professional lives. We want to feel pride in our accomplishments and shared success with our colleagues. We want to feel proud of the organization we're working for. If you're banking on plump paychecks alone to motivate your team and organization, think again.

Your other question at this point might be about value. Perhaps you're thinking, "What's the *commercial* benefit of giving work meaning?" Some people believe that if you can't measure it, it doesn't exist. By that standard, you'd never worry about something as intangible as vision. But ask Alan Lepofsky at Constellation Research and he'll show why that way of thinking is shortsighted. Alan has close to two decades of experience in the collaboration software industry, and his specialist research area is the future of work. When it comes to seeing fundamental value in a business, he looks for qualities that worked in the past that have been neglected in recent times. "Management needs to rekindle the spirit of great places to work," Alan says. "We need to convince executives that return on investment isn't the main measurement of the success of a project but, instead, employee satisfaction. When you have dedicated, loyal, loving employees, they will do more for your company than you could ever measure, as opposed to the last decade of whoever writes me the biggest check, I'll leave. That has to end."

Now let's be clear. This isn't about altruism. This is about making more money. Both Jon and Alan argue that you don't make a great business by simply paying people more. You *will* count the benefit of making work matter on the bottom line — thanks to the caliber of the people you recruit and retain, their high productivity, and the quality of work they do.

MAKE UNGLAMOROUS TASKS MATTER

The final stop on our search for meaningful work is understanding whether the mundane can feel like it matters. If you're saving lives, species, or the planet, it's not hard to see meaning in what you do. But some tasks suck; let's be honest. These are the tasks that seriously challenge motivation and vision. They're the moments when your team's instinct is to ask, *"Why on earth am I doing this?"* If you can't give them compelling answers, their morale sags and productivity ebbs away. But just think of the athletes sweating it out in the gym or training field for hours each day, or the movie stars memorizing their lines and floor marks, or even the Apollo astronauts who went back to school to brush up their calculus, algebra, and geology before reaching the moon.[6] Great athletes, actors, and astronauts find a way to give their best to the banal.

In the world of business, these tedious-but-necessary tasks most often take the form of paperwork and administrative duties. How can leaders make unglamorous tasks like these matter — or at least suck a little less? The answer lies in one of the unsung attributes of any motivated organization: transparency. Companies like Zappos have made transparency a core value of their organization.[7] To make unglamorous work matter, the challenge is to be transparent about what's being done, by whom, and why. This happens in five key areas.

1. Vision Transparency

To start, the vision of your organization must be transparent: clear, consistent, and well understood inside and outside the business. And, as author and consultant Simon Sinek has explained, the best visions start with clarity about *why* you're doing what you're doing, not just what you're doing or how.[8]

"If you hire people just because they can do a job, they'll work for your money," Sinek says. "But if you hire people who believe what you believe, they'll work for you with blood and sweat and tears." That's the level of commitment you're aiming for.

2. Objective Transparency

If colleagues don't know what they're trying to achieve, how will they know if they're succeeding? And if they can't define what success looks like, motivation will be elusive. The way to prevent colleagues from falling into a spiral of self-questioning doubt about whether they're doing the right thing is to be absolutely clear about what the right thing is. "My role can't matter if I don't know the objective."

3. Team Transparency

Similarly, team activity needs to be transparent. Colleagues have no need to wonder if everyone is working as hard as them or fielding the same burden of tedious-but-necessary tasks if they can see what everyone is doing and their own work is equally open to scrutiny. "I can't know my role if I don't know what others are doing as well."

4. Task Transparency

If folks don't see the point of what they're doing and how it fits a wider pattern of tasks, they'll always struggle to feel motivated. This might sound simple, but for the last five years running, Workfront's own research has shown that too much of the work week is soaked up with "shadow work" — tasks that seem to bear no relation to what you were hired to do. Just 40 percent of employees' time is spent on their primary duties, while interruptions, unproductive meetings, and administrative tasks eat up more than 27 percent.[9] Task transparency means clarity of expectations and requirements for each activity. "It is impossible for me to be proud of my work unless I can actually see it getting done."

5. Customer Transparency

Vision, objective, team, and task transparency combine to create accountability as well as a sense of purposeful action in the workplace. But work is given greater meaning when it is understood in the context of the final beneficiaries — how customers feel about the final product or service. Are they delighted or disappointed? Accountable transparency means understanding how your work contributes to customer satisfaction, feedback, and retention.

Now you may be thinking, "Nice idea, but no one is entirely transparent with customers about how a project or order is going until it's done." Well, talk to Dave Randall at Atlas Copco, the global industrial tools and equipment business. After seeing the benefit of giving more internal teams live access to the status of work in progress, Randall's team opened up that same insight to his customers. "I'm convinced that the more transparent we become with customers, the more information we give them — good or bad — the more trust we will build," says Dave. That's a principle worth following.

FINALLY, EMBRACE THE SUCK

There's a final essential ingredient in this recipe: honest communication. JFK didn't hide that America was behind in the space race, nor did he hide the technological challenges or the cost of putting people on the moon. Transparency helps us see where we fit and where our tasks fit within a broader pattern of work. The most tedious task becomes more meaningful, but it still may really suck to wade through it.

The slang term from the military, "embrace the suck," means to consciously accept or appreciate something that is extremely unpleasant but unavoidable. As a leader, be honest. Yes, the task is dull, but it needs to be done for all the reasons colleagues can now see. The job of the leader isn't to misrepresent or oversell. You'll win more respect by being open and realistic while painting the broader picture of what's at stake.

Creating a culture of transparency that helps to make work meaningful requires work tools geared for clarity and accountability. Tasks must be defined, progress must be tracked, team activity must be accessible, the end goal must be clear, and customer feedback must be open to scrutiny. Rather than spreading this information across different documents, formats, and platforms, gather it all in one place — an operational system of record, for example — and not only will those tedious-but-necessary tasks suck less, your team will also find greater meaning, motivation, and productivity in their daily work.[10]

That's your opening play as a leader, whatever your field of endeavor. You've got to make work matter. And if you're the leader of the work, only you can give it meaning. Irrespective of how big or small the task, keep in mind that "where there is no vision, the people perish."[11] It's old advice — more than 2,000 years old — but it holds true. Everything that follows in this book — from goal-setting, planning, building momentum, through to dealing with adversity — needs to be built on the bedrock of meaningful work. Whoever you are, whatever you're working on, you always need to believe — and help others believe — that your work matters.

Vision Statement

Compose a vision statement to bring meaning to your work

Does your team know the "why" behind their work? Do they believe that it matters? Use this worksheet to evaluate an existing vision statement or to write a new one.

STEP 1: WRITE YOUR VISION STATEMENT HERE, OR COMPOSE A NEW ONE.

_____

_____

_____

_____

_____

_____

STEP 2: TEST YOUR VISION STATEMENT.

Evaluate your vision against the elements of organizational belief outlined in the chapter. Answer each question below using a 1-5 scale.

1= not at all, 2= maybe a little, 3= neutral/not sure, 4= probably/likely, 5= definitely

HOPEFUL	1-5
Does your vision statement reflect your hope for the future?	
Is it optimistic enough to appeal to the dreamers in your organization?	
Is it pragmatic enough to appeal to the realists in your organization?	
Total your points and divide them by 3. Record the average here:	

POINTS BEYOND THE LEADER	1-5
How strongly does the vision apply to each of these groups?	
Team	
Organization/Company	
Community	
World	
Total your points and divide them by 5. Record the average here:	

EXTRAORDINARY	1-5
Does your vision statement "shoot for the moon"—stretching beyond your team's comfort zone?	

ATTAINABLE	1-5
Do you believe this can be done?	
Do you have time on your side to execute it?	
Do you have money on your side to execute it?	
Do you have skills on your side to execute it?	
Have you or anyone else accomplished something like this before?	
Total your points and divide them by 5. Record the average here:	

CLEARLY COMMUNICATED	1-5
Does your vision statement engage people emotionally?	
Does it engage people logically?	
Can each individual see how it applies to them and their role?	
Is your vision statement posted or shared in an accessible space?	
Do you refer to your vision statement often—verbally and otherwise?	
Total your points and divide them by 5. Record the average here:	

STEP 3: PLOT YOUR POINTS

Take your score or averaged score from each category, and plot it on the corresponding spoke on the radar chart below. Draw a circle through each plotted point to reveal the shape of your vision statement.

If your plot looks like the irregular circle in the middle, identify the attributes you need to focus more attention on to snap your vision into shape.

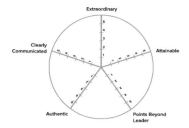

STEP 4: REVISE AND REFINE

Repeat steps 1-3 until your vision resembles the outer circle—achieving that perfect mix of optimism and pragmatism that leads to extraordinary results.

2

Who Do You Serve?

"You may be an ambassador to England or France...
but you're gonna have to serve somebody, yes indeed,
you're gonna have to serve somebody."

—BOB DYLAN

Imagine you can call on the advice of three titans of the business world. You want to ask a simple but fundamental question. *Who comes first: shareholders, employees, or customers?* Who takes priority? Whose star do you navigate by?

The first titan to respond to your question is the British entrepreneur Sir Richard Branson, founder of the Virgin Group, and he tells you:

"My philosophy has always been, if you can put staff first, your customer second and shareholders third, effectively, in the end, the shareholders do well, the customers do better, and you are happy."[12]

Sounds great! Everyone is happy if you put employees first, right?

But then you notice the two other titans shaking their heads.

Jack Ma, founder of Alibaba Group, one of the world's biggest technology conglomerates, leans forward. Ma says: "We believe customers are number one, employees numbers two, and shareholders are number three … I believe if the customer is happy, employees are happy, and the shareholders will be happy. But if shareholders are happy, it may not necessarily mean customers are happy and may not mean your employees will be happy."[13]

But that's plain wrong, says your third titan, Warren Buffett, Chairman and CEO of Berkshire Hathaway. Buffett tells you, "Directors should always act as if there is a single absentee owner and do everything reasonably possible to advance that owner's long-term interest."[14] Given that he bought his first stock in 1941 at age eleven and went on to become one of the most successful investors of all time, Buffett makes a compelling case for pursuing shareholder interests above all. The Oracle of Omaha has spoken; the priority of all businesses is "to please the owners."[15]

All three titans count their success in billions of dollars. They all oversee a varied portfolio of global businesses. Who is right?

The Branson-Ma-Buffett debate is a false choice. There isn't a perpetual struggle being played out in your boardroom between competing beasts — shareholders, customers, and coworkers — where one will win and lead the pack. Instead, you need to think of them as the mutually supporting ecosystem of your business. One constituent can't thrive without the others thriving too. Every piece of work you take on has a customer, teammates who do the work, and someone who pays for it. These are your stakeholders, and stakeholder analysis will guide the journey you're going to take them on, from how they see your organization today to how you want them to see you tomorrow. Let's be clear: What stakeholders think isn't just the concern of business titans like Branson, Ma, and Buffett. It's an issue for everyone in the business, wherever they sit on the org chart.

In this chapter, I'll explain how a change in mindset will enable you to run a simple three-step exercise in stakeholder analysis with your team.

We'll also explore two business stories that show what happens when you align the interests of customers, employees, and shareholders.

FIRST, CHANGE YOUR MINDSET: "PAST, FUTURE, PRESENT" THINKING

Before I explain how to carry out effective stakeholder analysis, we need to change the way we think about time. The human brain is flawed: We think about what happened in the past, and we spend today trying to fix yesterday so that we can get to tomorrow. This is linear thinking: *past, present, future*. And it's wrong. You can't fix anything that happened in the past. Working today to fix yesterday is a complete waste of time.

But you *can* fix where you're going. The better approach is to think about where you've been, where you want to get to, and how you can shape today to reach where you want to be tomorrow. You need to think: *past, future, present*. This simple but fundamental change of mindset will focus you and your stakeholders on forward progress rather than getting mired in an endless cycle of trying to fix past mistakes. This mindset change is the first step in getting stakeholder analysis right.

THE THREE-STEP EXERCISE

I joined a company with a great employee culture when I came to Workfront, but not enough was known across the organization about what our investors expected of us and what our customers were doing with our software. What problems were customers trying to solve? And could we engineer better solutions? We've been on a journey since then to add a customer-obsessed culture and a discipline of meeting and exceeding financial goals to an amazing team culture. Our starting point was a simple exercise:

1. Our team came together with a heap of sticky notes. I asked each person to write what our customers say about our company today and stick the notes on the wall. We repeated this for employees and shareholders. The result was a series of insights from our team about where we were on that day.

2. Then I asked our team to write down what they want customers, employees, and shareholders to say about the business in three to five years' time. Again, they stuck the notes on the wall. We now had insights into where our team hoped the business would go in the future. These insights were collated into a future state description of our company as seen through the collective eyes of our customers, our employees, and our shareholders.

3. Finally, we developed a communication flow that consolidated our future state vision into a simple statement: "When we create a category called modern work management and bring the operational system of record to market, our shareholders will say that we are reliable in creating a return for them, our employees will say that Workfront was one of their favorite career experiences and our customers will say that we were genuinely interested in their success."

This statement served as a compass when we went through the exercises you will see in Chapters 3 and 4. Our stakeholder filter created four priorities, and we were able to tell our stakeholders how our four priorities would benefit them. These four priorities became the basis for our company goals for several years: Achieve Sales and Marketing Excellence, Become a Product-Driven Company, Activate the Ideal Customer Experience, and Cultivate a Contagious Culture. We now had a recipe for alignment of interests as the company moves forward.

That's *past, future, present* thinking in action. In the space of a couple of hours, you'll have a practical plan for how to align and advance customer, employee, and shareholder interests. I have run this same exercise hundreds of times over twenty-five years, and I've always landed on a great outcome. Sounds too simple? This exercise gives people the opportunity to see that their concerns and ideas are like their teammates'. If you believe, as I do, that the answer to any question lies within your team, you can save time and energy by just asking them. The wisdom is in the room. All you need to do is tap into it.

Nowhere is this clearer than in the stories of Dräger and Purple Mattress.

STORY #1: ALIGNING CUSTOMER, COWORKER, AND STAKE-HOLDER INTERESTS

In the early 2010s, Claudia Brozda at Dräger weighed some challenging feedback from three customers. Dräger has a proud record of innovation — more than a century of experience in creating lifesaving critical-care technologies you'll find in clinics and hospitals around the globe. Think of devices that monitor breathing in neonatal units or intensive care, or maybe patient monitoring tools in operating theaters or monitoring devices at a patient's bedside on a ward. That's Dräger. But these three customers all seemed to be saying the same thing: something was going wrong with implementation.

"They said our teams were so focused on what they had to do, the customers felt a little pushed out of the way. It was all about the checklist, the to-do list," Claudia explains when I ask her what the feedback was. This wasn't the company's guiding philosophy. Dräger has always taken pride in having an intimate knowledge of customer needs.[16]

As senior director for Professional Services, Claudia spent time with each customer to explore their concerns more deeply. Then she set about re-engineering Dräger's approach, calling in help from two experienced implementation teams. "We're too internally focused. Let's figure out what's important to the clinicians in the hospitals and clinics we're working with," Claudia told them. "And let's think about what those clinicians have to do with *their* customers — the people at the end of our medical devices."

Claudia's decisive leadership play — the adoption of customer-focused implementation, or CFI as she called it — took a year. But the result was an alignment of customer and employee priorities. That's not all. Reflecting five years later, Claudia describes a wider pay-off for the business. The benefits are felt in growing customer satisfaction and retention, and opportunities to create new products and services. Dräger's deep understanding of customer needs is helping to drive innovation. New telemetry and mobile monitoring products and services have been created, allowing medical staff to keep track of patients who need care but no longer need to be hooked up to a bed. New technology is also being developed to combat "alarm fatigue" — the constant warning beeps from different devices — to help nurses differentiate between informational alerts and emergency alarms. Put plainly, Dräger's financial stakeholders are seeing their business grow thanks to a successful alignment of customer needs, the company's products, and coworkers' approach to implementation. It's a true win-win-win situation. "This is the three-legged stool in business," says Claudia. "I'm a firm believer in creating balance."

Perspective

Claudia Brozda makes a simple but sharp observation about how our perspectives shift as we progress in our careers:

"You want to be an expert in your chosen discipline at the beginning of your career and focus on developing your expertise. Then, as you progress, you start thinking more about colleagues and customers. As you mature in your career progression, you start to understand stakeholders and what's driving the company to be successful. You have to start balancing those different groups and understand how to align them."

Don't make the mistake of thinking that when you move up the rungs of the career ladder you're giving up interest in what you were doing before — and whose interest you were serving. And that raises another question of perspective.

As the modern work leader in your organization, you are chief steward of the ecosystem of customers, employees, and shareholders. I believe there are two types of leaders in the world. One leader wakes up in the morning and asks, "What are people going to do *for me* today?" The other asks, "What *am I* going to do for people today?" The latter is playing the role of servant leader.[17] They see leadership as enabling others to do the job they were hired to do. They clear obstacles on the road ahead. They are motivators when times are tough. And they strive every day to maintain the

> forward momentum of their team.
>
> Your perspective on leadership is your choice. What kind of leader will you choose to be?

STORY #2: WHEN A BOOST IN BUSINESS THROWS THINGS OUT OF ALIGNMENT

What connects Goldilocks, a raw egg, and tens of millions of people around the world? The answer is a viral video commercial created by Purple, the US company which claims to have reinvented the way mattresses are designed. Purple wasn't always in the business of sleep. Back in the early 1990s, the company was making high-tech carbon-fiber wheelchairs. But customers let them know that the standard wheelchair cushions they were sitting on were far from comfortable.

This sparked the Purple team to investigate the science of comfort and the development of a breakthrough material for cushions and mattresses, initially for the healthcare sector. By the early 2010s, Purple had developed an innovative manufacturing process that allowed them to branch out of specialist healthcare supplies towards the broader consumer mattress industry. But the traditional routes to market — distribution agreements and retail stores — didn't work as they had hoped. So, they decided: "Let's go digitally." Cue actress Mallory Everton and her performance as a mischievous Goldilocks who demonstrates the "just right" quality of a Purple mattress.[18] The mattress became an overnight customer hit. And that's when Purple's challenge began.

According to Charlie Smith, the company's chief operating officer, "We had fifteen to thirty employees for twenty years, and all of a sudden, from January of 2016 to January of 2018, we grew to 900 employees." The speed of their success put the business out of balance.

Shareholders were happy and customers were hungry for Purple's products, but even though the team was growing rapidly, it was struggling to keeping pace. At one stage, the production team even asked the marketing team to stop generating demand! Charlie took a step back and realized that the best way to align the interests of all stakeholders was to create a new company-within-a-company. The new company deployed a shared work management platform, so everyone could see what was going on. There were fewer surprises, more synchronicity. Purple's story underlines how leaders need to always have an eye on stakeholder balance — even when business is booming.

ALIGNMENT ISN'T ALWAYS AGREEMENT

As we wrap up this chapter, let's zoom in on one stakeholder group for a moment: employees. A common leadership mistake is to think alignment equals agreement all the time. It doesn't. It takes debate and disagreement to create a healthy ecosystem in your organization. The question is, how do you harness debate for a positive outcome? In their 2010 book, *The Right Fight*, business strategists Saj-Nicole Joni and Damon Beyer concluded that leaders are too preoccupied with running a happy, harmonious ship. Leaders are not concerned enough about how constructive disagreement can bring creative energy to a business.[19] This isn't a case for starting all-out war between coworkers: it's a recognition that sometimes dissent and debate are worth encouraging. The leadership challenge is to know how to fight the right fights. Helpfully, Joni and Beyer set out six principles that guide leaders to fight well:

1. Make the fight material. The benefit to the business has got to be big enough to justify the argument.

2. Focus on the future. Blame about past mistakes doesn't carry a business forward.
3. Only fight for a noble purpose. This could be customer care or investing in your team.
4. Establish rules. You want a managed boxing bout rather than total war.
5. Structure formally; work it out informally. Set up the fight within your organization's chain of command but work out tensions informally.
6. Turn pain into gain. Make sure everyone benefits, including those on the losing side of the debate.

Joni and Beyer say that playing by these six ground rules for a right fight gives organizations a chance to reduce decision-making risk, create value through innovation and change, and grow better leaders. I said a little earlier that the answer to most questions already exists in the "wisdom in the room" — the knowledge, experience, and expertise of your team. Put that idea together with Joni and Beyer's six principles, and there's an essential task for any leader. You must create a climate where constructive debate and disagreement can tease out the best answers to whatever questions you face — at every level of the business, not just the boardroom.

BACK TO THE FUTURE?

"In the end, shareholder returns are just an outcome of management practices that respect all constituencies," wrote Professor Jeffrey Pfeffer of Stanford University in 2009.[20] The professor looked back to a golden age of leadership in the mid-twentieth century when "CEOs saw their role as balancing interests." This was partly driven by CEOs understanding their job as "stewards of the valuable resources entrusted to them," and partly by understanding that each group was "essential for organizational success." The professor concluded, "What was true then is even more so today, in an age of knowledge work, outsourcing, global supply chains, and activist interest groups."

Being a steward of valuable resources is not just for the CEO. If you lead any type of work in your organization, this is your chance to get it right.

Start by gathering the team. Then take a heap of sticky notes and play out the three-step stakeholder analysis. You'll have the recipe for balance, and you will have the basis for the communications and decisions required on your journey, all of which will set you up to pinpoint the single most important thing you can do, as we'll see in the next chapter.

Service Statement

Align the interests of customers, stakeholders, and staff

How healthy is your business ecosystem? This exercise will reveal how three groups of stakeholders see your business today, so you can better influence how they see it tomorrow.

In this self-driven constituent analysis, you'll document, analyze, and align the interests of your:

- Shareholders — those who fund the work
- Employees — those who do the work
- Customers — those who are impacted by the work

Note: This is a simplified version of the six-step exercise you read about in Chapter 2. Depending on the needs and size of your team, you can follow either approach to align constituent interests and ensure you're always focusing your efforts on the right work.

STEP 1: DOCUMENT THE PRESENT.

Write down what each constituent group says about your company today, what they like, what they want, and what they need.

CONSTITUENT	WHAT THEY SAY ABOUT US TODAY
Shareholders *Fund the work...*	
Employees *Do the work...*	
Customers *Impacted by work...*	

STEP 2: IDENTIFY COMMON INTERESTS.

Go back to the table you just created and circle areas of overlap, looking for areas where interests converge.

STEP 3: CREATE FUTURE STATEMENTS.

Focusing mostly on the areas of overlap you discovered in step 2, write down the things you'd like shareholders, employees, and customers to say 3-5 years from now.

CONSTITUENT	WHAT WE WANT THEM TO SAY ABOUT US IN THE FUTURE
Shareholders *Fund the work...*	
Employees *Do the work...*	
Customers *Impacted by work...*	

STEP 4: SIMPLIFY IT INTO A SINGLE SENTENCE.
THIS IS YOUR NEW SERVICE STATEMENT.

Look for overarching themes and use them to identify your top 3 action items or goals that will take your company into the future while balancing the needs of each group.

When we accomplish our work, our shareholders will say _____

_____ ,

our employees will say _____

_____ ,

and our customers will say _____

_____ .

3

Harness Commander's Intent

"The height of my goals will not hold me in awe,
though I may stumble often before they are reached."

—OG MANDINO

"Whatever anyone else says, the single most powerful leadership concept is Commander's Intent," says former US Navy SEAL Commander Mark McGinnis. Commander's Intent has guided him throughout his distinguished military service as one of only four in US military history to move from the Marines to the SEALs. Today, Mark brings his experience and inspiration to bear on the businesses and leadership teams he works with around the country. His belief in Commander's Intent is about clarity of purpose and articulating the end goal. But, as he explains, it's also about letting teams deploy their expertise.

Mark says, "As a leader, I'm going to communicate what we're trying to accomplish and why, as well as what the battle space is going to look like when the gun smoke settles." He adds, "At that point, I'm going to get out of your way and let you figure out how we're going to get there. You're the expert."

Commander's Intent acknowledges what is easy to overlook when you're leading a team: you don't need to have all the answers. You just need one clear answer: what you're trying to achieve. Mark explains that SEAL teams have a tremendous amount of aggregate wisdom. Collectively, the team will have much more experience than a single team leader. They're trained in a variety of disciplines. These days, the chances are they will have studied at Wharton, Harvard, or the Kellogg School of Management, as well as taking part in special operations around the world. The team leader, for all their strengths, is likely to have far fewer years of experience to draw on than the whole team.

"The best leaders," Mark says, "are the ones who figure out real fast that they have unbelievably talented people working with them, and if they just point them in the right direction, give them enough information, put them in positions that play to their strengths, and shield them from their personal weaknesses, the likelihood of success goes way up."

In this chapter, we explore why you need to encourage your team to own their solutions. We then look at four types of goals, including what distinguishes an extraordinary goal from a pipe dream — and how to prevent your work from becoming a nightmare. Finally, we'll discuss ways you can encourage your team to push for the extraordinary, all with the power of your intent.

Commander's Intent at Workfront

Commander's Intent for the leadership team at Workfront has the attributes that Mark describes: clarity of outcome underlined by some specific expectations and clear constraints too. Here's what it looks like:

The executive leadership team at Workfront, consisting of the direct reports to the president and CEO of Workfront, will lead an enterprise SaaS company to create modern work management as a category by delivering an enterprise application platform that serves as a company's operational system of record.

The single most important thing this team can do is to create and keep customers.

The team will accomplish their objective by achieving sales and marketing excellence, becoming a product-driven company, activating an ideal customer journey, and cultivating a culture that is contagious.

Operational constraints include our long-term target-operating model of greater than 30 percent ARR growth, 90 percent gross renewal rates, 120 percent net renewal rates, and achieving the "Rule of 40."

All of this must be accomplished within the cultural boundaries of getting it done and doing it right.

ENCOURAGING YOUR TEAM TO OWN THEIR SOLUTIONS

Mark describes an essential truth about leadership and human nature. If a leader trusts a team to solve the problem they all face, then the team owns the solutions and will be more invested in securing successful outcomes. It's a truth that echoes through history. You'll find a similar sentiment by the Athenian general Alcibiades in Steven Pressfield's novel *Tides of War*. Alcibiades says,

> If I command you, "Pick up that bowl," and set a swordpoint to your back, you will obey, but no part will own the action. You will exculpate yourself, accounting, "He made me do it, I had no choice." But if I only suggest and you comply, then you must own your own compliance and, owning it, stand by it.[21]

I saw the same defense-defiance-determination reflex in my eldest son, Will (now twenty-two), who would declare as a toddler: "I do it by Will!" In a similar vein some years later, Will challenged one of the basic parenting instincts: to protect a child from making mistakes. He demanded, "Who are you to deny me the mistakes I need to make to determine who I am to become?"

However young or old, we don't like being told what to do. But we do like being asked to help (preferably not at swordpoint). You might think that leadership lessons from a US Navy Seal Commander with twenty-five years of operations behind him — or an ancient Athenian general, for that matter — are a little remote from your own experience or the needs of your organization. Think again. You may not be leading life or death operations, but the concepts of Commander's Intent and voluntary compliance can be applied to any leadership role in any industry. Keep in mind the key lesson: ensure that the purpose and parameters of the mission are clearly understood, then trust your team to deliver the actions to get you there.

Your first step is to give up chasing the heroic ideal of leadership that's so engrained in popular culture, the ideal where a charismatic leader takes charge at a decisive moment. Sure, leaders should step forward at points of crisis, whether they're in a combat theater, a courtroom, a laboratory, a classroom, or a conference room. But your organization shouldn't be in constant panic mode. So, take off that cape and cowl. Trust your team.

Remember how you felt as you were making career progress? You didn't want to always look up the chain of command or management for answers. The same applies to your team. Everyone wants to be trusted to do the job they were hired for. Good ideas exist at every pay grade. The leadership challenge is not to answer every question, but to listen out for them and, most importantly, involve others in setting the right goals.

UNDERSTANDING THE FOUR TYPES OF GOALS

A mentor of mine, Art Wilson, taught me how to set goals effectively. He was one of the top sales leaders at IBM for more than two decades and went on to co-author the book, *Building a Successful Selling Organization*. Along with everything I've seen in my career, talking to Art has convinced me there are four types of goals.

Four Types of Goals

1. **Clear Goals.** The team is confident they can achieve these initiatives by working the way they work today. They're likely to be reruns of previous tasks or projects — more of the same.
2. **Stretch Goals.** These goals are likely to be variations of familiar tasks or working patterns that will challenge and push the team —a more intense version of the same.

3. **Extraordinary Goals.** These are the audacious objectives you and others deeply desire. They're at the edge of your headlights, and they will require you to *change the way you are working today*. Everyone on the project will learn something from the project — and they will all experience time outside their comfort zone.

4. **Pipe Dreams.** These ideas are so far away from reality that no one believes they're possible. Pipe dreams tend to take two forms: the unattainable growth fantasy or the unachievable savings scenario.

Here's a Shootman Law of Leadership: When your team is striving toward an extraordinary goal, chances are they will hit clear and stretch goals along the way. Even if they fall short of the original extraordinary objective, your organization will have made significant progress — progress that goes beyond what most businesses would expect. Of course, you must protect against your team getting despondent when they don't always accomplish the extraordinary. Leaders need to make sure that what *has* been achieved gets celebrated.

But before you decide to push *every* goal into extraordinary territory, there are wise voices counseling you to exercise caution. Kathy Haven, VP and director of strategic operations at the global advertising and marketing agency FCB, is one such voice. Kathy suggests there are two key variables when deciding how high to shoot:

1. Have you got the right mix of talent?

"The first thing is finding the right team to successfully implement the plan," says Kathy. "Hopefully, you'll have committed advocates on your team who will work hard to align other people and work creatively to make the project a success. Finding committed advocates is a key step towards achieving the extraordinary." Extraordinary goals will push your team to think and act in new ways. But your team must have the core competencies required to fulfill the brief. They need the right attitude too! And as Kathy suggests, if you don't have the right talent-and-attitude mix at hand, an extraordinary goal will be out of reach.

2. How much change is already happening in the business?

"If there's a lot of other change happening at the same time, it may not be the right time to push for the extraordinary," says Kathy. There's a limit to how much complexity the human brain can process and engage with emotionally. Asking your team to push for too much change all at once can transform extraordinary goals into pipe dreams. That means time, money, and energy could go to waste.

Kathy is right. To give your team the best chance of achieving something extraordinary, you need to think about timing, talent, and your wider business context. If the timing looks right and you've got the right people in the team, push for extraordinary goals.

CASE STUDY: WHEN PIPE DREAMS BECOME NIGHTMARES

Kathy also tells a cautionary tale about a pipe dream that became a nightmare: a two-year software deployment that lasted more than ten years.

The project started with good intentions. The idea was to deploy a single software tool across the whole organization that everyone would use. Great idea! The *right* software combined with the right implementation can have a transformative effect on a business. But this software had been designed for manufacturing industries rather than service organizations. "Even the terminology was a huge turnoff," says Kathy. "We worked in an office, but the software called it a plant." The leadership had picked a good tool, but for someone else's business. Kathy says, "None of the users wanted this, from the chief financial officer to the receptionist who greeted everybody at the front door. It just was hard to use, clunky, and didn't fit our business."

Sounds like the team was chasing a Pipe Dream. There was a well-intentioned belief that a *one-size-fits-the-entire-business* technology would create efficiencies. That's an honorable intention. But the solution must be flexible enough to adapt to everyone's needs. If not, the project will misfire, and the benefits won't materialize. Listening to the wisdom within the team would have saved time, money, and most certainly sleepless nights. The key lesson? Ask.

Kathy says, "I typically will start off any project — whether it's a deployment or a process improvement — by asking users, 'Why are we doing this?' and 'What's in this for you?'" As Kathy aptly points out, if the answers that come back are vague, that's a red flag. You're likely talking about a pipe dream rather than a project with tangible and clearly defined goals where the benefits are understood. The key to any successful project is engagement — not at the end of the project, but at the outset.

A simple stress test

I use a five-minute stress test to distinguish if the team believes they are pursuing an extraordinary goal or a pipe dream. It's adapted from an exercise in the bestseller *How Did That Happen?* by business consultants Roger Connors and Tom Smith. In the book, the authors explained there's a difference between team alignment and "mere complyment."[22] Leaders need to know people are fully behind a plan, rather than simply going along with it. Connors and Smith suggest asking your team to score on a scale of one to ten their level of agreement with whatever you're planning to do. That will give you a snapshot of their overall confidence. Below five? Your team may understand why they are pursuing the goal but have real doubts about the "how." Six to eight? They generally agree it might need some additional debate and then will move forward with both their hearts and their minds. Regardless of the score, you can always improve it by encouraging follow-up discussion.

You need to pinpoint the source of your team's concern or lack of alignment. People may be uncommitted for a variety of reasons, but you can generally get their concerns to the surface by asking deeper questions in four categories:

1. Is it clear? Is the task or project well-defined?
2. Is it achievable? What's the confidence level in getting this done?
3. Is it needed? Is this task or project necessary?
4. Is it linked? Does it fit with the wider strategic priorities of the business?

I recently gathered our fifty top leaders in a room and asked the Connors and Smith question, "On a scale of one to ten, how do you agree with what we're planning to do?" The result: a 7.8. The score, which we shared publically, led us to conduct a full day off-site meeting for those leaders: an off-site that dramatically improved our chances of executing well. As Connors and Smith explain, "Once you pinpoint what is missing, you can set about resolving any concerns."

ENCOURAGING YOUR TEAM TO PUSH FOR EXTRAORDINARY GOALS

Now, for all of us Alcibiades wannabes, it is time to transfer ownership of our goals. Let's imagine a conversation between a leader and a team:

"What do you think we can achieve next quarter?" asks the leader.

A team member defines what they think the team can comfortably achieve at the existing run rate of activity and with existing resources.

"So, if we work the same way, but just push harder with what we've got, what does that outcome look like next quarter?" asks the leader.

Another team member starts to define a stretch goal.

"What do we really want to happen? What would be an amazing outcome, one in which everything went as well as it possibly could? Where do you think we would end up?"

The team members start to define what an extraordinary goal looks like.

"But, of course, boss, to do that, we'd need x resources, y expertise, and z experience in the team," they say.

This simple dialogue gives you a definition of what good, great, and extraordinary outcomes look like, plus an indication of resourcing requirements. No need for rousing speeches. Yes, you can leave that copy of Shakespeare's *Henry V* or the collected speeches of Abe Lincoln on the shelf. Save the heroic words for another day.

A conversation like this also gives you a barometer reading of the mood, aspirations, and concerns of the team. You understand them a little better. And they will see you as a leader who is interested in what they think and what their talents can achieve. If they seem to be lacking in energy and morale, you can start to see what the root of the problems might be. We'll develop ideas about good communication techniques in later chapters (particularly Chapters 6 and 7). For now, this kind of goal-setting dialogue will help you with buy-in — with the added benefit of insight into team sentiment. You'll find effective leaders using this collaborative approach across different industries.

Take Alison Angilletta, PMO director at RWJBarnabas Health, the largest healthcare system in the state of New Jersey. Says Alison, "A manager has a different perspective than somebody who's doing the daily work. And what the manager thinks will work might be done or approached a different way by someone on her team. So, you must act collaboratively — it's the most comprehensive and achievable way to create goals."

Collaboration about goals gives you certainty from the outset that you're not creating a Pipe Dream, and that those you lead own their solutions — no sword needed. You're not persuading them; they're persuading you. From here, they can start to break down the steps and resources needed to achieve the extraordinary goal. Specific tasks, timelines, and milestones can be defined, documented, and shared. That's where we're heading next. But before we do, here's your new leadership challenge. Stop trying to persuade people to hit an extraordinary target and *let them tell you* how they'll do it. Choose an area where you want the business to excel. Now play out the goal-setting dialogue with your team. The more you do it, the better you'll be at it. Remember the five-minute stress test to be sure you're aiming for the extraordinary rather than a pipe dream so you can actually achieve your Commander's Intent. And remember, if falling short means hitting a stretch goal, you have nothing to lose and everything to gain.

Commander's Intent
Clarify and communicate what you're trying to achieve

As we learned in this chapter, commander's intent is about clarity of purpose, articulating the end goal, and then giving your team space to deploy their expertise through goals. These elements are key:

- Outcomes
- Key Activities
- Operating Constraints

ACTIVITY 1: FORMULATE YOUR COMMANDER'S INTENT

Write a commander's intent for your team that aligns with your vision statement (Chapter 1) and service statement (Chapter 2). Divide your commander's intent into four parts, as shown here. Fill out parts 1, 2, and 4 now. Save part 3 until after you read Chapter 4 and complete Exercise #4.

PART 1: THE CLEAR OUTCOME OF ACHIEVING OUR PURPOSE LOOKS LIKE...

PART 2: THE SINGLE MOST IMPORTANT THING THIS TEAM CAN DO IS...

COMPLETE AFTER
EXERCISE #4

PART 3: THE TEAM WILL ACCOMPLISH THEIR OBJECTIVE BY...

PART 4: OUR OPERATIONAL CONSTRAINTS INCLUDE...

TIP: Refer back to the commander's intent for Workfront's leadership team, found in the sidebar early in Chapter 3.

ACTIVITY 2: PRACTICE SETTING EXTRAORDINARY GOALS

The purpose of defining your commander's intent is to give you a North Star—something with which to align your key initiatives and extraordinary goals, which we'll set in Chapter 4. But first, I want you to practice going through the process of defining clear, stretch, and extraordinary goals, so you can build that muscle.

STEP 1

Select an area of your personal life that you're trying to improve, such as health, physical fitness, or finances, and write it here:

_____

STEP 2

Write one goal of each type, making sure each is written in the form of a *measurable outcome*.

CLEAR GOAL A measurable outcome I know I can accomplish, because I've done something similar before.	EXAMPLE *I will run for 15 minutes a day, 3 days a week.*	YOUR TURN
STRETCH GOAL A measurable outcome that will push me to a new level of intensity.	EXAMPLE *I will alternate 5 minutes of running with 1 minute of sprinting for 30 minutes a day, 3 days a week.*	YOUR TURN
EXTRAORDINARY GOAL A measurable outcome that will push me out of my comfort zone and require me to change the way I do things today.	EXAMPLE *I will run/sprint for 30 minutes a day, 3 days a week, adding 5 minutes every week, until I reach 60-minute sessions.*	YOUR TURN

TIP: Don't forget to apply the five-minute stress to make sure your extraordinary goal isn't a pipe dream.

4

Plan and Achieve Extraordinary Goals

"Plans are worthless, but planning is everything."

—DWIGHT D. EISENHOWER

A college student in Austin, Texas, learned valuable business lessons while waiting tables at Houston's Restaurant in the 1980s. The restaurant was owned by George Biel, a man who knew what made a great meal. It wasn't just the ingredients. And it was more than the quality of the cooking. Biel believed a great meal was the whole experience from the moment the diners walked through the door to the moment they stepped back out at the end of their dinner. Guests needed to be greeted within thirty seconds of taking their seat at a table. Within two minutes, they'd be served their first round of drinks. If each course of the meal took too long to prepare and serve — more than fifteen minutes — there was an apology from the manager. If the kitchen was really running late, the meal was free of charge. If a dish were sent back to the kitchen because it wasn't cooked to perfection, the guest who sent it back would dine for free. If it was sent back a second time, none of the guests at the table would pay for their meal. Even the time it took to deliver the check and take payment was measured against the clock.

This wasn't fast food; this was calm and efficient service. Diners rightly thought they were getting a great experience and delicious food, but the restaurant's close attention to timing also meant it could accommodate an extra table turn each night. Biel had broken down an exceptional experience for customers into a sequence of key steps for his team, each of them easy to understand. He had set a timeframe for action. And he had defined what the best next actions should be if things didn't go quite to plan. Everyone working at Houston's could feel customers' happiness at the end of a perfect meal — and you could count it in the tips! Staff continually circulated around the restaurant. If a waiter passed a table that needed clearing, it was cleaned up regardless of who was dealing with those customers. Everyone was invested in quality service. Likewise, everyone felt the disappointment when things went wrong. Sure, it was hard work, but there was an emotional investment in success and failure. That young waiter paying his way through college classes in the '80s, learning how to define and deliver extraordinary service time after time, was me.

Everything I've seen in my career since tells me that George Biel had it right. Whatever the field of endeavor, there's a pattern of activity that helps to deliver extraordinary results. You can take Biel's principles and apply them to whatever you need to do. You'll have noticed that one key feature of his approach was measurement of activity, which we'll investigate in a later chapter. In this chapter, we're going to explore the characteristics of successful plans and how to plan for extraordinary results. But first, we need to look inside your head.

THE ELEPHANT, THE RIDER, AND THE PATH

It's no accident that Biel's approach worked. He may not have thought it out this way, but his methods were tuned to how our brains appear to be wired. Psychologist Jonathan Haidt uses the metaphor of an elephant and a rider to illustrate this concept. According to Haidt, our emotional brain is like an elephant and our rational brain is like a rider sitting on the top.[23] We persuade ourselves that the rational rider is like a "charioteer with a firm grip on the reins." Our cool, collected, thoughtful self is always in charge, right? But the elephant is made up of our instinctive selves: "Gut feelings, visceral reactions, emotions, and intuitions." The elephant is wired to act instantly to perceived threats and pleasures. The rider is thinking of the long-term. As Haidt wrote in his best seller, *The Happiness Hypothesis: Finding Modern Truth in Ancient Wisdom*, "The elephant and the rider each have their own intelligence, and when they work together well they enable the unique brilliance of human beings. But they don't always work together well."

When the elephant-like emotional self decides to stampede, the rational rider has little control over the direction or destination. "We sometimes fall into the view that we are fighting with our unconscious, our id, or our animal self," Haidt argues. "But really we are the whole thing. We are the rider, and we are the elephant. Both have their strengths and special skills."[24] If you want people to engage with something, you need to appeal to both their rational *and* emotional side.

How does this metaphor apply to planning? Well, brothers Chip and Dan Heath took Haidt's thinking about psychology and applied it to the field of change management in their book *Switch*. I was fortunate to get to know Chip, a professor at Stanford Graduate School of Business, about a decade ago when I was working at Eloqua and he served on our advisory board. Along with his brother Dan, a senior fellow at Duke University's CASE center, he has created a three-part framework based on the elephant and the rider concept[25]:

1. **Direct the rider.**
   "What looks like resistance is often a lack of clarity. So, provide crystal-clear direction."
2. **Motivate the elephant.**
   "It's critical that you engage people's emotional side — get their elephants on the path and cooperative."
3. **Shape the path.**
   "If you want people to change, you can provide clear direction (rider), or boost their motivation and determination (elephant). Alternatively, you can simply make the journey easier. Create a steep downhill slope and give them a push. Remove some friction from the trail. Scatter around lots of signs to tell them they are getting close. In short, you can shape the path."

Chip and Dan also highlight the need to make a plan digestible for everyone involved, particularly because human brains struggle to get emotionally enrolled in complex issues and tasks. They advocate for "shrinking the change." You need to help everyone understand where they are now, where they're headed, and the route they're going to take. And you need to make sure people think *and* feel it matters — that there's a rational and emotional payoff.

That's precisely what George Biel did at Houston's Restaurant. Everyone had clarity of purpose, felt emotionally engaged in each night's service, understood the path of activity ahead of them, and believed it mattered.

With the psychology of planning and motivation in mind, let's see how this foundation applies to another business that's producing extraordinary work.

PLANNING THE TREK WAY

Sean Pederson poses a simple challenge to designers or product developers when they approach him with new ideas: "Try to define the problem you're trying to solve in one sentence."

As the engineering product manager at Trek Bicycles, Pederson oversees the process of taking a concept from the drawing board to the road. Exceptionally high standards are expected by Trek in everything they do. I know this because I am the proud and satisfied owner of four of their bikes! The founders, Dick Burke and Bevil Hogg, chose the name in the 1970s because it "held the promise of longevity and freedom and exploration and quality."[26] One of the company's guiding philosophies is "the best service is no service." In other words, what reaches the cyclist is as near perfect as the company can possibly make it. It's not going to break. It's not going to spend time back in the shop. You're buying the best you can buy, and it's going to last a lifetime — a promise that's baked in to every project Pederson manages.

For Pederson, it all starts with finding that single sentence to guide the project. As he said in our conversation, "Oftentimes, you can start mapping out a goal, and it becomes three, four, five sentences. And from that, you find that you're just creating more problems for whatever you're trying to solve. So, when I'm leading a team and we're talking about establishing a new process or planning out the design and development of a new product, I try to lead the team down the path of 'keep it simple.' One sentence: define it. And one question: is it measurable?"

Don't go to Pederson with a vague aspiration such as "build me the sexiest bike ever." And don't go with a pipe dream such as "let's build a hover bike." The question is, *what extraordinary but attainable goal can we accomplish here and now*? "Fundamentally, it all revolves around simplifying," says Pederson, whose approach can be broken down into three simple principles.

1. ***Objectives should be specific without being too descriptive.***
   "Avoid rambling, ambiguous statements that can have multiple interpretations. This adds complexity to what should be a very simple statement."

2. ***Objectives must be measurable.***
   "Time and time again, I find myself in the position of being the one to raise my hand and say, 'How do we measure success from what you're asking for? How do we know we've accomplished that goal?' This is all in line with helping the team create direction and forward momentum — just helping them understand what a specific, measurable milestone looks like."

3. ***Objectives need everyone's emotional buy-in — minus the drama.***
   "The last thing, and this is probably the biggest one for me, is about maintaining momentum for projects: Leave any drama at the door. We're all passionate about what we're doing here, and we have a common, shared cause. But sometimes individual opinions differ. It's our role as a leader, as a project manager, to help teams and team members connect emotionally to what we're trying to do — even if what we're doing is not exactly what they want."

Of course, not everything always goes to plan (read on to Chapter 8 to discover the story of how Pederson and the Trek team overcame obstacles to create one of the company's signature products: the Bontrager R Flare taillight). But, for now, you can hear echoes of George Biel, Jonathan Haidt, and Chip and Dan Heath in Pederson's words. Success is all about simplicity, clarity, and channeling passion in a positive way — ensuring that coworkers' emotional connection to a project points in the direction you're all headed.

MIRROR MOMENT: WHY YOUR BRAIN STRUGGLES TO EMOTIONALLY ENROLL WITH COMPLEX OR LARGE-SCALE PROBLEMS

Here's a quick personal test of how your brain engages — or doesn't — with complex emotional issues. Think about the last time you dug into your pocket and gave serious dollars to charity. I'm not talking about a few coins in a collection jar. The chances are you did so because you were spurred to act by small stories. Charitable organizations are trying to save communities, cure diseases, and conserve species. But when you donated — or even volunteered to help — did you feel like you were making a difference to one person or one family, or whole communities? Did you feel like you were supporting sick children or trying to cure a disease? Did you think you were supporting efforts to return an orphaned animal to the wild or save an entire endangered species? At what scale did you see your generosity playing out?

We feel horror when we hear of mass casualties and suffering, but such stories ultimately bring a sense of impotence. We're more likely to act when we hear individual stories of someone's loss or their survival against adversity. To put it crudely, we buy relatable stories about "someone who could be me" or "like someone I know" ... or, more powerfully, "someone I aspire to be."

Note that if you're looking for a great cause to donate to or volunteer with, you'll find information about two charities at the end of this book.

THE THREE COMPONENTS OF PLANNING FOR EXTRAORDINARY RESULTS

What I've described so far are the characteristics of a successful project, which is great on a conceptual level. But how do you translate simplicity, clarity, and emotional engagement into a practical pattern of activity that will deliver extraordinary results?

Planning tends to be an expansive process. You usually start from a simple point — the definition of a strategic objective — and then try to encompass every possible eventuality and option along the way. But the better model is contractive. Break your extraordinary goal into key initiatives, milestones, and best next actions. For each, you need to answer the following questions:

1. What's going to be done?
2. Who owns it?
3. When will this be done?
4. What does "done" look like?

Key initiatives

Key initiatives are projects or actions that take an organization closer to its goals. These might be intended to improve the operational efficiency of the business, fuel innovation, address challenges from competitors, or adapt to changing market conditions.

At Workfront, I ask teams starting a project or program to take part in a sticky-note exercise that builds on the sticky-note exercise in Chapter 2. First, using the future state of our stakeholders as a compass, team members write down all the things that could possibly be done to move towards our agreed upon goal. Second, the team gets split into two or more groups and is asked to take a share of the sticky notes from the wall and sort them into clusters of related tasks or themes. Invariably, you end up with four to six clusters of ideas. Those clusters are potential key initiatives. What you'll find is that one or two of the clusters look the same — have the same associations — across all the teams. That means the "wisdom in the room" has identified what really matters. After some voting and "right fights" we get the entire team to a point in which we have three to five key initiatives.

Milestones

We then take key initiatives through the extraordinary goal-setting process and break each key initiative down into smaller actions called milestones. As the name suggests, these are the steps along the way, helping to show how far you're moving towards completion of each key initiative. To create milestones, ask, "If we did X, do we have just barely a chance of accomplishing the key initiative? If not, what's only one more thing we need to do?" After hundreds of these exercises, I have found that every time the key initiative breaks into no more than four to six milestones. Note that these do not necessarily get captured in sequential order. They're merely the major items the team will need to work on and likely will be worked on simultaneously.

Why you should barely accomplish your milestones

The culture of most organizations is that every task needs 100 percent effort. Wrong. Every task needs 100 percent completion. When you're 99 percent of the way there, all you need is an extra 1 percent to sign off a job as complete, not an extra 10 percent or more. When we give ourselves permission to *barely accomplish* tasks, we can get more work done, much more quickly. So keep this simple sequence of events in mind: just barely get it done, celebrate the completion of that phase of work, and then move on to the next task, phase of work, or project.

As British psychologist Tony Crabbe advises, you need to "downgrade perfectionism." Crabbe is a research fellow in organizational psychology at Birkbeck College, University of London, and his expertise has been called on by the likes of Microsoft, Disney, News Corporation, and Salesforce.[27] According to Crabbe, workplace perfectionism is often a symptom of a lack of trust between coworkers and management. Coworkers try to second-guess what will please their managers and the folks higher up the chain — and they do more work than is necessary as a result. "In the absence of trust, we overengineer to protect ourselves, and we drive towards perfection," Tony says. "It takes a lot of courage to barely accomplish." But that's what you need to do: set clear milestones and encourage your team to barely accomplish them as they drive towards the extraordinary goal.

Best next actions (BNA)

The crucial delivery of an extraordinary goal is a focus on the best next action. At heart, a BNA is a simple question or pair of questions with a bias towards action:

"What are we going to do next?"

"What's the one thing we're going to do within the next two weeks that will take us closer to a milestone?"

You're not inviting answers with multiple possibilities. You want to hear about the one action that matters most right now. And channel your inner Alcibiades: it is what *they think* they can get done, not what you tell them.

At this point, you've started with a broad perspective — represented by a seemingly random array of notes on a meeting room wall — and broken it down into where we're going next. We've not just got a plan, we've got a plan of action.

How do BNAs work in practice? Let me tell you a story of a Shootman family challenge. When one of my kids turns fourteen, their challenge is to climb one of Colorado's "fourteeners" — a mountain 14,000 feet high or more. When my son Sam turned fourteen, we spent seven hours climbing a peak called Mount Quandary. At 12,000 feet, Sam sat down in a heap and said he couldn't go on. "Okay, well, let's just try to reach the cairn over there," I said, pointing to one of the many small stacks of rocks serving as a marker along the trail. Sam carried on. At each trail marker, we stopped, took a break, and set reaching the next trail marker as our next goal. At 700 feet short of the summit, Sam said,

"Dad, I'm done." The air was thin, and he was tired. "Sam," I said, "just look behind you — see how far you've come. All you've got left is 700 feet." So, he picked himself up and reached the top. No one can ever take away the satisfaction on his face when he looked down from the summit of Mount Quandary.

What's the moral of this story? We broke down what seemed to be an impossible goal into best next actions. And we celebrated successful momentum at each milestone. Sam now has a story of extraordinary achievement that tells him he can accomplish far more than he imagined possible. In fact the following year he challenged me to summiting two 14ers in one day.

An example plan

To put this in perspective, I thought I'd share with you an example output from some work with my team from a couple of years ago. Once we did our stakeholder analysis we developed four key initiatives: Achieve Sales and Marketing Excellence, Become a Product-Driven Company, Activate the Ideal Customer Journey, and Cultivate a Contagious Culture. Below you will see the original key initiative, milestone, and BNA plan for Achieve Sales and Marketing Excellence. This is copied straight from our notes at the end of that day. From here we created an easier-to-digest document, but everything that happened next stemmed from these original notes.

I. Achieve Sales and Marketing Excellence

Measures:
1. Achieve new and growth ARR targets.
2. Achieve CAC payback of less than eighteen months.

II. Milestones

1. Define targets and develop framework for investment thesis for top of funnel performance.
   Done = Achieve cost per qualified sales opportunity targets.
   Owner = Mike
   Two week goal = Define first three marketing actions to improve top of funnel.
2. Establish methodology and targets for the revenue engine.
   Done = Achieve velocity, value, and conversion rate targets.
   Owner = Joe
   Two week goal = Meet with Carl and capture his thoughts on the process framework.
3. Develop and implement new segmentation strategy.
   Done = Product, marketing, sales, and delivery agree.

Compensation and targets are aligned to the defined segmentation strategy.

Owner = Joe

Two week goal = Complete definition of net new customer segments.

4. Sales execution plan aligns with customer segmentation and product plans.

   Done = Develop, get stakeholder buy-in, and publish the plan. Evaluate the success of the plan.

   Owner = Carl

   Two week goal = Meet to understand the draft of the sales plan.

5. Marketing execution plan — Aligns with customer and product plan.

   Done = Develop, get stakeholder buy-in, and publish the plan. Evaluate the success of the plan (the plan will add a section on rhythm, structure, and mix).

   Owner = Joe

   Two week goal = Create the structure of the plan and share with sales.

6. Define indirect go-to-market model.

   Done = Develop, get stakeholder buy-in, and publish the plan. Evaluate the success of the plan.

   Owner = Paige

   Two week goal = Brainstorm Workfront value prop to partners.

THINKING, FEELING, AND STRUCTURED ACTION

What we've explored is how the combination of thinking, feeling, and structured action can help to achieve objectives. By focusing your efforts around a pattern of successful activity — including a limited number of clearly defined key initiatives, milestones, and best next actions — you'll have broken down the complexity of your work into something coworkers can rally around. That extraordinary goal you've all agreed on now appears to be a sequence of achievable steps. Those elephants and riders within every member of the team will see the path ahead, have a sense of how quickly they need to travel, and know what they need do to reach each marker along the way. You've helped them believe that they're embarking on a noble journey. You've given them a map. All they need to do is start walking.

Key Initiatives

Break your goals down into concrete components

You've formulated 3/4ths of your commander's intent. You've practiced setting clear, stretch, and extraordinary goals. Now you need to "shape the path" by creating a practical pattern of activity for your team to follow.

PART A: IDENTIFY KEY INITIATIVES

STEP 1: INVITE EXPANSIVE THINKING
Gather your team, hand each person a stack of sticky notes, and set a timer for a couple of minutes. Share parts 1 and 2 of your commander's intent from Exercise #3, and ask everyone to write down as many ideas as possible for accomplishing them—one idea per sticky note—and to stick them to the wall in a random order.

STEP 2: INVITE CONTRACTIVE THINKING
If you have a large group, divide them into two teams, and invite each team to take half the sticky notes off the wall and group them into 4-6 clusters or themes. These are your potential key initiatives. (You'll have some leftover ideas that don't fit into a theme, and that's okay.)

STEP 3: IDENTIFY YOUR KEY INITIATIVES
Ask each team to present their 4-6 clusters or themes. You'll find that one or more of those clusters will be very similar across the two teams, making them key initiatives front runners. Use the wisdom in the room to identify other clusters or themes that should become key initiatives as well. Write your final key initiatives in the chart that follows.

KEY INITIATIVE #1:	
Extraordinary goal (measurable outcome):	
Owner:	Date:

KEY INITIATIVE #2:

Extraordinary goal (measurable outcome):

Owner:

Date:

KEY INITIATIVE #3:

Extraordinary goal (measurable outcome):

Owner:

Date:

KEY INITIATIVE #4:

Extraordinary goal (measurable outcome):

Owner:

Date:

KEY INITIATIVE #5:

Extraordinary goal (measurable outcome):

Owner:

Date:

PART B: MAP YOUR MILESTONES

What works for climbing a 14,000-ft. peak also works for accomplishing a key initiative. Select ONE key initiative from Part C that you'd like to break down into milestones. Remember, your goal is to create the smallest possible plan.

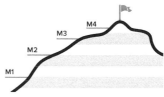

Rewrite the key initiative here:

_____

_____

STEP 1: LIST MILESTONES

Ask your team, "What is one thing we will have to do for sure to meet the extraordinary goal for this key initiative?" Include it as a milestone below (M1, M2, etc.). These are the big rocks you have to move, and they will all move at different rates and paces—not necessarily sequentially.

STEP 2: BARELY ACCOMPLISH

Pause after each milestone and ask, "If we stop there, will we just BARELY achieve the key initiative?" Circle NO or YES. Keep adding milestones until you hit your first YES. That's your last milestone.

M1: _____ NO / YES

M2: _____ NO / YES

M3: _____ NO / YES

M4: _____ NO / YES

M5: _____ NO / YES

STEP 3: EVALUATE

If after five milestones, you find you still haven't hit a YES answer, then you aren't working at a high enough level.

PART C: DETERMINE YOUR BEST NEXT ACTIONS

So you have a key initiative identified, and you've divided it into no more than 4-5 Milestones. You've now shaped the path that your team will follow. Now you need to determine how to navigate along that path. That's where best next actions come in.

STEP 1: BRAINSTORM YOUR BEST NEXT ACTIONS
Take each milestone and write down a few actions you are confident your team can accomplish in the next couple of weeks.

STEP 2: ADD DETAIL
Determine what "done" looks like for each BNA, and assign each one an owner and a date. Do this for each milestone. Your BNAs do not have to be sequential, and you can work on BNAs for several different milestones simultaneously.

STEP 3: START KNOCKING OUT YOUR BNAs
The secret to activating momentum and direction is insisting that the current BNA gets done and then relentlessly refocusing on one new BNA (but not ten) at least every couple of weeks.

PART D: FINALIZE YOUR COMMANDER'S INTENT

Flip back to Exercise #3, Activity 1, where you started formulating your commander's intent, and complete Part 3 "The team will accomplish their objective by..." with a brief summary of the key initiatives you just identified.

_____
_____
_____
_____

5

Direction and Momentum

"Everyone has a plan 'til they get punched in the mouth."

—MIKE TYSON

"I'll take you back to when I was coaching my oldest in baseball, and we were teaching the boys running the bases," says Kevin Ellington, leaning back in his chair. "We'd get the fastest two boys on the team and ask them to run from me to a tree. They were about the same speed. Then we moved one of them about ten feet behind the other and told the one in front, 'We're going to start him, and as soon as he passes you, you take off.' Every time, even though those boys could run just as fast, the one who started behind reached the tree first. He had momentum."

Kevin defies easy description. He's been a pastor, a firefighter, a master brewer, and he remains a committed outdoorsman. Today, he's director of transformational services at enterprise change consultancy LeapPoint. The same laws of motion he described in baseball training apply to business. Just like gravity pulls you back to Earth and friction slows you down, the physics of business is full of forces that hinder progress. Organizations with momentum in a marketplace win, and teams with momentum achieve the best results, regardless of who started ahead of them or how far behind they were at the beginning.

It is not likely that your work plan will survive its first encounter with reality. Your primary responsibility as leader is to create and maintain direction and momentum. How do you do this? How do you relentlessly focus on direction and momentum? And once you can see a team making progress — how do you help them maintain it? That's what we'll explore in this chapter.

CHECK SIX: PRECONDITIONS TO ACHIEVE MOMENTUM

You will have noticed three themes running through the first half of this book: clarity, simplicity, and breaking down the complex into the digestible. We've explored how these themes apply to making work meaningful, balancing constituents, determining what to do, and planning. They are crucial to achieving momentum too. You won't win a race if you're standing on the starting line, wondering why you're there, where the finish line is, or what to do next. But you need something more than clarity — you need coworkers and chemistry. You need to be sure you're starting with what's needed to get the job done. You need to ask:

1. Do I have the right people to get this done?
2. Do they have what they believe is necessary to hit this goal?

To achieve the extraordinary, your team needs to have the right mix of talents and access to the right resources. If something is missing from the mix — whether that's technical knowledge, contacts, or character — momentum will elude you. And you can't skip the chemistry step. As we'll see later in the chapter, if you don't have the right mix of talent and personality from the start, the project has a strong chance of going awry. There's a helpful phrase that fighter pilots use that's also great leadership advice: "check six." This means look behind you. Are the people following you the right people — and do they have everything they need? If you're clear, you're ready to get started and build momentum.

WHAT LEWIS AND CLARK CAN TEACH US ABOUT ZIGZAGGING MOMENTUM

The ancient Greek mathematician Archimedes said, "*The shortest distance between two points is a straight line.*" But that's not what modern work is like. Momentum in business is rarely a relentless forward movement in a straight line. Sure, the concept of running from Point A to Point B at full tilt, like Kevin's base runners, might be fine for simple tasks with a clear goal. But more complex projects and long-term strategic objectives are seldom easy and never straightforward. The unexpected will do its best to knock you off course. When the British Prime Minister Harold Macmillan was asked by a journalist in the late 1950s what would change the course of his government, he replied: "Events, dear boy, events."[28] History is full of examples that show momentum isn't linear. Those who achieve the extraordinary more often follow a zigzag of gradual progress as the prevailing winds change.

You'll hear an interesting take on momentum if you head over to the offices of Viasat — a company in the vanguard of digital and mobile communications, from introducing next generation in-flight high-speed broadband on commercial flights to military satellite communications in the field. Viasat's senior director of IT, Scott Shippy, puts a modern twist on a familiar story from US history: the Lewis and Clark

Expedition to explore the lands west of the Mississippi from 1804 to 1806. Scott says, "Can you imagine, in today's culture, Lewis and Clark trying to get to the Pacific Northwest? They would go up a stream; they would find a dead end. They'd turn back; they'd go another way. Today, we would say, 'We should turn back, or get a new leader — do something different because we didn't meet our objectives along the way.'" He believes that today's problem is that teams are too tied to the original plan they created. When a specific tactic isn't achieved, teams get discouraged and doubt their leaders. "But the worst project manager in the world is one who sticks to the plan," says Scott. "The worst leader in the world is the one who doesn't change the plan. When the straight path isn't working, do something different."

You're always looking for the best next action, but the vigilant leader sees each BNA with a full range of motion best captured by an old Turkish proverb on the wall in Scott's office in Colorado: "No matter how far you have gone on the wrong road, turn back."

I've seldom seen successful projects hit their objective by dashing full tilt in a straight line. There's always been a zigzag en route. But to zigzag, you and your team must be vigilant for signs that you need to take an alternative path to your extraordinary goal. And that raises the questions that keep leaders awake at night:

1. How do you know when it's time to change course?
2. How do you know you're making the right decision?
3. How do you decide between different possible routes?

Two people from very different walks of life can help us with the answers.

KNOWING WHEN IT'S TIME TO CHANGE COURSE: GO/NO-GO CRITERIA

Back in Chapter 3, former US Navy SEAL Commander Mark McGinnis introduced the concept of commander's intent. His advice was to have absolute clarity about the end goal. But you'll remember that Mark also said that once the goal was set, "I'm going to get out of your way and let you figure out how we're going to get there." How do the SEALs make critical decisions during missions? How do they decide whether to press on with Plan A to achieve their goal or stop, rethink, and take another course? According to Mark, it's all about *go/no-go criteria*.

The SEALs run missions through five phases: insertion, infiltration, actions on the objective, exfiltration, and extract. The mission is carefully planned to include contingency arrangements and what commander's intent looks like at the end of each phase. The final planning stage is to determine the go/no-go criteria. These are "hard and fast rules" and anyone in a leadership role on the mission during any phase can make the call to continue or abort. Says Mark:

> It could be as simple as a timeline: The commander needs eyes on a target by a certain day and time. If the terrain is so treacherous, we've underestimated that in our planning process, and we know that we're not going to get to the target by that certain day and time, we've got a couple of options. We can ask for a Rolex — an extension of that time. Maybe they'll allow it. Or maybe it's a hard and fast: "No, and if you can't get there we've got to figure something else out." We bake go/no-go criteria into everything that we do.

Mark is describing a simple equation. Can you still reach your goal with the team, tools, and resources in the time you had planned and in the context of the terrain you face? A complex problem is stripped back to a clear binary choice: yes or no. Crucially, the criteria are established in the cool of the planning room, not in the heat of the battlefield. There's no chance for emotions to cloud good judgments. You can apply the same principles to your leadership decision-making. At *every point* in a project, you need to decide if your team still has what's required to reach the objective. Can the extraordinary goal still be reached if a key team member suddenly left the business, for example? What happens if market conditions change and create a less favorable climate than at the start? Go/no-go criteria will help focus your thinking on what the best next action should be.

WHAT'S YOUR COMPASS-POINT QUESTION?

If Mark's go/no-go advice gives you a framework for deciding whether a plan needs to change, then how do you choose the best alternative route? Business decisions are rarely a choice between Option A and Option B. There's usually an alphabet of possibilities. Business psychologist Tony Crabbe told us in the last chapter about the need to downgrade perfectionism. But Tony also suggests a simple way of determining what's the best next action: what I'll call a *compass-point question*.

He tells the story of the British Men's Rowing Eight who won gold at the Sydney Olympics in the year 2000.[29] These eight athletes were clear on their end goal: to cross the finish line first. But how to win was a series of choices about optimal training, diet, race planning and tactics, and the technology of the boat and oars. All eight crewmen had opinions about the right approach. When those opinions differed, the men rallied around a single question: "Will it make the boat go

66

faster?" This became their decision-making compass — a question that always kept them looking towards their extraordinary goal. Tony has found that many organizations aren't clear on their goal, whether that's improving customers' situations or driving innovation. "Getting more clarity over what's the fundamental goal is helpful," he says. "Having a common decision-making framework provides a language for people to engage with these conversations."

Now, I'm not a rower, and there's no Olympic gold medal on display in my office. But I've always found that a compass-point question can be a quick way to focus attention on what we're all trying to achieve. It gives the team a way to debate options and recommend a course of action that isn't based on personalities or pay grades — only the right way to reach the goal. If you look back at the Workfront commander's intent you'll see our compass-point question right in the middle, *"Is it going to help us create and keep customers?"*

A compass-point question and a best next action make a powerful combination. The compass-point question helps to keep everyone focused on the agreed upon strategy. The BNA questions — *"What are we going to do next?"* and *"What are we going to do within the next two weeks to take us closer to our goal?"* — will guide your tactical decisions en route to the goal.

We've established that good progress doesn't always follow a straight line. We've got a method to determine whether we need to rethink (go/no-go). And we've got a mechanism for deciding what direction to take if we need to zigzag (a compass-point question). But there's something else to watch out for. You need to watch out for dysfunctional momentum.

HOW TO AVOID DYSFUNCTIONAL MOMENTUM

Energy, drive, and focus all sound like the magic ingredients that will make any project fly, right? Well, sometimes momentum can carry a team away. Academics Kathleen M. Sutcliffe and Michelle A. Barton have described a phenomenon called "dysfunctional momentum." This is when there's so much focus and commitment that there's no room for critical thinking. Writing in *MIT Sloan Management Review*,[30] Barton and Sutcliffe suggested there are five reasons that momentum can go awry:

1. Overreliance on action
2. Inflexible planning
3. The ripple effect of small changes
4. Rationalization of information that invalidates what they expect
5. Deference to expertise of others — particularly those with more power/status

According to Sutcliffe and Barton, "To overcome dysfunctional momentum, you need to do the one thing you are least likely to want to do in the middle of a crisis. You have to allow yourself to be interrupted, or else create the interruption yourself." This underlines another benefit of using BNA questions to help maintain momentum. There's no chance of inflexibility if the question is always, what are we doing next? You're baking in regular points to reflect on progress and next steps.

The best defense against the observations of Sutcliffe and Barton is to combat dysfunctional momentum in the first place rather than attempt to overcome it once it has taken hold. When most folks develop their resource plan they only think about the skills or talent necessary to staff the work. But I'd argue chemistry is the most important element to getting stuff done. At Workfront, we understand our personality mix by using the Insight Discovery Wheel, a psychometric test which assigns a color palette — from fiery red to cool blue — to different character types.[31]

1. Red = Be brief. Be right. Be gone.
2. Yellow = Involve me.
3. Blue = Give me the details.
4. Green = Show me you care.

We're each a mix of attributes but tend to have a prevailing personality trait. The best part about this test is that it doesn't care if you're male or female, what your race is, or your creed. As a result, you can objectively create balance on your team.

A simple test I've run countless times underlines the need for balance. In an off-site, I'll ask all the reds, blues, yellows, and greens to work in their color group to build a person out of Lego bricks against the clock. The single-color teams sometime succeed but never beat the one team that is a mix of reds, blues, yellows, and greens. Sometimes the people least like us are the exact counterbalance to the worst parts of our own tendencies. I'm red: On a good day, I'm decisive and self-reliant. On a bad day, I'm impatient and hasty. Think a team with all reds could create dysfunctional momentum? Absolutely. This means the shy to the gregarious must find ways to collaborate. And when they do, their chances of overcoming obstacles increase. Getting the chemistry at the outset is essential — and the best way to keep momentum on the right track.

Two leadership behaviors that support momentum

Your job as a leader doesn't finish when you've given everyone clarity about what goal you're chasing and why. You need to support the team's ongoing efforts.

1. Be a snowplow.

Everyone's leadership style will differ in line with their personality. But as I stated in Chapter 2, the best leaders follow a servant mindset. You exist to help others do the job you've hired them to do. Or, as Amy Spencer, Chief of Staff & Senior Director of Strategic Marketing Services at Blackbaud, explains, "I'm the snowplow in front of the team." Amy isn't going to let obstacles on the path ahead get in the way of her coworkers' progress! If it's within your power to clear the terrain of potential obstacles, that's when you intervene.

2. Make time for micro-interactions.

Remember Alison Angilletta from Chapter 3? She advocates "micro-interactions": small, frequent conversations with coworkers to assess their confidence in the project at hand and as an early-warning system about emerging problems. Her answer to maintaining momentum? "Lots and lots of communication," says Alison. "What I've found is when you establish relationships with people, they are more likely to share with you. It's not about big, hour-long meetings where we'll go through every single project and every single issue. It's just a lot of micro-interactions. If something comes up and you need to talk for ten minutes? Let's talk for ten minutes. Or if I see you in the hallway, and I can tell that you're a little frustrated? I'll ask what's happening. It's just making it a very natural interaction." Never underestimate the power of a gentle, daily nudge in a positive direction.

The next chapter is all about the cadence of chasing progress — how leaders can find out what they need to know without putting people on the defensive or skewing attention away from what matters to achieve the extraordinary goal. But what Alison is describing is something simple, obvious. Be visible. Be available. If a team is working on an extraordinary goal — a strategic priority — let them see you are available to support decisions and clear obstacles out of the way. Embrace your inner snowplow driver!

GOOD LUCK!

So, your team has set off on its journey toward the extraordinary. You've given them clarity and simplicity, and you've made it all digestible. You have a kit bag of momentum-making tools — go/no-go criteria, compass-point questions, and best next actions — to help you make good and timely leadership decisions as the team works towards each milestone. Everything is in place to achieve momentum. And you're relaxed if the project doesn't run in a straight line to the goal; zigzagging is part of business life.

Your next set of leadership challenges pick up from Sutcliffe and Barton's advice to be vigilant for dysfunctional momentum. What's the best way for a leader to chase progress? What's the cadence for leadership communications? How do you talk to your team without fear or favor — and without diverting attention from what matters?

That's where we're heading next.

Check Six

Define your compass-point question and go/no-go criteria

As we learned in this chapter, momentum toward an extraordinary goal rarely progresses in a straight line. At this point it is time for a "Check six." It's a term fighter pilots use to refer to the 6:00 spot on the clock, which is directly behind you. This is your final quality check before you begin to manage the cadence of the work.

The two simple tools in this exercise will help you ensure that you have a tight plan and give you helpful language for discussing and altering the plan.

STEP 1: WRITE A COMPASS-POINT QUESTION

What is your guiding force? What is the one simple question that will always lead you back to your overall goal? (e.g., "Will it make the boat go faster?") Come back to this question at each decision point.

TIP: Flip back to Exercise 3, Activity 1, Part 2. Take your response to the prompt "The single most important thing this team can do is..." and rephrase it in the form of a question.

STEP 2: DETERMINE GO/NO-GO CRITERIA

Remember, this is the "Mission Abort" criteria for each milestone. For example, "If X happens..." or "If Y isn't approved/funded/developed/hired..." then you will try a different tactic. There are two simple tricks for discovering useful go/no-go criteria that will signify when it's time to re-group and steer in another direction.

- Look back at your BNAs, whether you wrote them on the Chapter 4 worksheet or somewhere else, and circle those that are absolutely non-negotiable.

- Identify a nightmare scenario for each milestone. Ask yourself, "What could happen that would make it impossible to complete this milestone?"

Using the insights from these two activities, write 1-3 go/no-go criteria for each milestone in the table on the next page.

KEY INITIATIVE:

MILESTONE 1:	GO/NO-GO CRITERIA:

MILESTONE 2:	GO/NO-GO CRITERIA:

MILESTONE 3:	GO/NO-GO CRITERIA:

MILESTONE 4:	GO/NO-GO CRITERIA:

MILESTONE 5:	GO/NO-GO CRITERIA:

TIP: Reflect on the compass-point question whenever you reach a no-go point. And remember the Turkish proverb on Scott Shippy's wall: "No matter how far you have gone on the wrong road, turn back."

6

Stay Focused

"Cross my heart and hope to die, taking this one step at a time.
I got your back if you got mine, one foot in front of the other."

—WALK THE MOON, "ONE FOOT"

When you work as a 911 call dispatcher, you're a listening witness to life's most challenging moments. You need solid, reliable information from people under stress — and you need it fast. You'll make critical decisions about injuries and incidents you cannot see, and you'll dispatch emergency responders to crime scenes or accidents you'll never attend. Call dispatchers master the art of asking the right questions in the right way. Reflecting on her career, Cynthia Boon sees her seven years working on 911 calls — first as a call dispatcher, then as a trainer — as a rich source of insight into dealing with people and making decisions. Today, you'll find Cynthia leading a strategic initiatives group on the North America Customer Experience team at General Motors Financial, one of the world's biggest auto-finance providers. Cynthia says, "One of the biggest lessons I learned was about what 911 call-takers call 300 Call Syndrome. That's when you take call after call about the same accident. But one of the calls that comes in — the 300th call — is about a different incident happening in the same place. You must be able to identify that. You must treat each call separately; you can't assume everyone is talking about the same thing. You have to get to the truth in each case."

Cynthia's story frames a vital skill every leader must master in striving to maintain their team's momentum: how do you ask questions that get to the essential facts fast? But there's a related question that's just as important: where do you focus your attention — how do you know what's a priority?

Throughout this book we've talked about how modern work is best done when everyone is clear about direction and can see meaning in their role and tasks. That makes clarity of communication vital. It also means that priorities should be clear. In this chapter, we'll explore two hard truths. Firstly, you'll never have all the decision-making information you want. How much information is enough? Secondly, everyone will always seem to be too busy. You're going to have to persuade them to let some tasks drop. Then we will explore how asking about the wrong thing can interrupt momentum and skew your team's priorities. And flipping that over, we'll see how asking about the right thing in the wrong way can demotivate your team and diminish the chances of achieving an extraordinary goal. Finally, we'll look in the mirror at how we can best respond under pressure.

Let's start with those two hard truths about decision-making and prioritization.

HARD TRUTH #1: DON'T WAIT FOR 100 PERCENT TO MAKE A DECISION

The leaders of today and tomorrow will have more data to guide their decisions than at any point in human history. As Eric Schmidt, former CEO of Google, once declared, "There were five exabytes of information created between the dawn of civilization through 2003, but that much information is now created every two days."[32] Technology is helping to identify patterns in performance that are beyond the sight and comprehension of human managers — patterns that are hidden in vast, complex datasets. And we've even started to mythologize data-based decision-making. The *Moneyball* story of how General Manager Billy Beane guided the Oakland Athletics to glory using data analytics to guide player picks has passed into both sporting and business legend.[33] But does machine learning, the advent of artificial intelligence, and the aggregation of data *guarantee* leaders will make better decisions? No — and it never will. Forty-two percent of respondents to a Cap Gemini/Economist Intelligence Unit survey of more than 600 global executives expressed concern over the complexity and time taken to interpret unstructured data. Opportunities whiz by as we try to wrangle the data.[34]

The alternative is what great leaders have always done: take the best evidence you can muster in good time and trust your gut. Former Secretary of State and Chairman of the Joint Chiefs Colin Powell calls it the P40/P70 rule. Secretary Powell says, "Sometimes what my analytical mind says to me is not what I'll do. Generally, you should act somewhere between P40 and P70, as I call it. Sometime after you have obtained 40 percent of all the information you are liable to get, start thinking in terms of making a decision. When you have about 70 percent of all the information, you probably ought to decide because you may lose an opportunity in losing time."[35]

Your aim is to make a good decision, not a perfect one. It's the counterpart concept to asking your team to *barely accomplish* a task: you need to know *just enough* to decide. Get comfortable with making decisions with less than 100 percent certainty. The leaders who win will be those courageous enough to make decisions without waiting for all possible information. If you've hit Secretary Powell's 70 percent, make a move.

HARD TRUTH #2: STOP EVERYONE BEING TOO BUSY

The second hard truth is about prioritization. Everyone you see at work is busy. You're busy too! There's wisdom in the words of academic, author of the best seller *Grit: The Power of Passion and Perseverance*, and nonprofit founder Angela Duckworth: "Gritty leaders are incredibly hard-working. But they're also lazy because they don't want to work on everything. In fact, they typically only want to work on one thing: the one thing they love. And everything else becomes a second priority."[36]

Angela makes it plain: "Leaders need to brutally prioritize their one thing above all other things, about which they should be really, infinitely industrious. But at the same time, they need to be lazy about everything else." Leaders must work on what matters and let the rest slide!

But what about their teams?

You'll recall that back in Chapter 4, British psychologist Tony Crabbe advised leaders to "downgrade perfectionism." Likewise, what Tony describes as *busyness culture* diverts attention from where it needs to be focused. Busyness is the culture of perpetual motion. Everyone feels there's not enough time to do the jobs they're paid to do, often because "shadow work" — the stuff that seems remote from our goals — eats up close to half of their time![37] Tony says people feel insulated against criticism when they appear to be busy: "You never have to justify working faster and harder and quicker. And that's why busyness is seductive."

But Tony's most recent research with the University of Utrecht in the

Netherlands is a lesson in how thinking about the best next action can help to beat the culture of busyness. Workers involved in his research typically had three priorities focused on monthly, quarterly, or annual objectives. But they weren't being translated into day-to-day action. Strategic priorities didn't even enter the workers' daily decisions on what to do. Tony now asks those workers to, effectively, focus on the best next action. He says, "What we're trying to do now is get people to insert a question before committing their time: 'Should I check my email now or go to that meeting?' or 'Which is more valuable: working on my three goals or spending a couple of hours in a meeting?' It then becomes a meaningful choice." Over time, I expect Tony's research will show that thinking about day-to-day actions in the context of strategic goals will increase productivity, results, and the velocity of action.

Outside academia, you'll find companies trying different ways to beat busyness. Tony points to what's happening at Facebook and Google as examples of how companies are trying to create a culture where people feel empowered to *not* get everything done. For example, at Facebook, managers are starting to set "non-goals" — calling out what their team will not do while they focus on achieving strategic objectives.

Don't accept the prevailing culture of busyness. Strive to create a more trusting culture where coworkers understand that putting an extraordinary goal first and letting go of shadow work is a good choice.

WHERE SHOULD LEADERS FOCUS THEIR ATTENTION?

Let's imagine you've persuaded your team to drop perfectionism and resist unproductive shadow work. And let's assume you're making *just good enough* decisions in line with Secretary Powell's P40/P70 rule. Every day, you'll find me asking a couple of simple questions geared toward maintaining momentum:

"What do you think we should do next?"

"What do you think we can achieve in the next week or two?"

You'll also find me looking at a simple dashboard that shows current progress toward our key initiatives and confidence in achieving extraordinary goals. If milestones are being met or exceeded and progress towards completion is on track or ahead of schedule — within the resources allocated to the project — then it's achieving *escape velocity*. That bird is flying. That's where I encourage and release rather than investigate. If milestones are being missed, progress is falling behind schedule, and additional resources are being spent, that's where I know I need to spend time and attention. That bird is grounded and needs help to fly.

ASK THE RIGHT QUESTIONS

Being a questioning leader can prove to be a blessing or a curse to projects. One of Shootman's Laws of Leadership is, "What the leader is interested in, people will be fascinated by." In other words, asking the right questions at the right time can create necessary focus in grounded projects. You can use your power for good. But the *wrong question* can accidentally focus team members' attention on tangential matters. Before you know it, a casual expression of interest in a topic morphs into, "The boss wants to know about ..." and teams begin diverting time and focus into feeding that interest.

I learned this lesson the hard way. Here's the story. We name our conference rooms after clients, and I once casually mentioned that it would be great to decorate the room with one of their signature products. I imagined something recycled or salvaged, not the $5,000 bill that followed to have a new product made up in our brand colors! Since it was my fault we bought this item. I found myself reimbursing the company thousands of dollars for an unnecessary expense. It was my mistake, I owned it, and I learned from it. I'm now the proud owner of a top-of-the-line item, custom-built in our corporate branding, and it looks really good in my garage. I tell this story to illustrate how easy it is for a simple misunderstanding to divert resources from what's most important. If this can happen with a side conversation about conference room décor, it can happen in strategy meetings about key initiatives too.

Stick to the story your dashboard tells you! The dashboard will highlight the work that requires a nudge to regain momentum — and where the right questions from a leader will focus the team's fascination on the right things. But successful leadership isn't just *what* you ask, it's *how* you ask. That's where we're headed next.

THE RIGHT WAY TO FRAME QUESTIONS

"I'd say I'm on my fifth career," quips Erica Gunn as she charts her progress from a nonprofit trade organization in Washington, DC, to teaching in a middle school in the Bronx, to a software company, to the Bill and Melinda Gates Foundation. Today you'll find her working as a vice president at a major fashion retailer in the Pacific Northwest. Her varied experience has given her sharp insight into effective communication and how to adapt her own "super direct" style to suit different audiences. "I work really hard every day to think about how I say things and how that impacts the results I expect to get," Erica says. She describes a common temptation among leaders. It's that urge to say, "*No, no, no. I've seen this one before. I know what happens here.*" Says Erica:

Somebody I work with and really admire almost never says, "Why didn't you do that?" or "Why didn't that happen?" Instead, he asks questions.

"Where do you think we are now?"

"Is that where you think we should be?"

"What do you think the next steps ought to be to get us to where you think we should be?"

"What do you think the next action should be?"

I really try to change my style, when I'm working through challenges, to be more curious and questioning.

Erica is describing neutral communication. It's the same tone as my two everyday questions: *"What do you think we should do next?"* and *"What do you think we can achieve in the next week or two?"* It's stripped down language: bare of emotion, guilt, blame, or praise. There's no room for caveats or tentative "maybes." You want to know what's happened and what's happening next. And, crucially, you want to hear the answers come from the team or the individual. No top-down diktat from the boss. There's a vital difference between this and asking someone, "Why hasn't this been done?" and "Why haven't you done this?"

On the one hand, when you ask, "Why hasn't this been done?" you're identifying problems with the work underway. On the other, you're implying blame. A better approach still: "How likely is this to get done?" or "What quality of work do you think is happening on this?" This switch to neutral language moves dialogue from potential conflict towards a more positive discussion of the best next action.

Be aware that the bigger the gap between you and the people who are doing the work — the more intervening links in the management chain — the more neutral language can help. When people worry that a leader is looking at them and their work with a critical eye, there's a temptation to deflect blame. Neutral language removes the temptation. And, as Erica Gunn says, inviting people to describe how they would solve a problem can inspire them and empower them. "Even if the leader knows the answer — because they've done it 100 times before — they shouldn't give the answer. They should ask for participation and ask leading questions that get to the right outcome."

Neutral language paired with encouragement to participate is a powerful combination. Right now, you'll find neutral conversations happening in modern work teams across the globe — short, focused conversations that are rooted in a belief that the folks in the room have the right combination of talents to fix whatever needs to be fixed. Talk to Philip Stickland of Adventist Health System, and you'll hear him describe running daily scrums with his team that quickly determine what's working and what the obstacles are to progress. "I know I can run through a daily list of tasks that are 'done, doing, will do, and blocked' with my team in ten minutes," says Philip. "They know what I expect, and they know that I respect that they can do what needs to be done."

The Accountability Question

How did that happen? It's a question every leader will ask at some point, and it's the title that business consultants Roger Connors and Tom Smith chose for their book about how to hold people accountable for the work they do, as we highlighted in Chapter 3. Connors and Smith set out three principles — the accountability assumption, the accountability fallacy, and the accountability truth.

These principles remind us that: (a) most people want and aim to do a good job; (b) failure to accomplish tasks is a different problem than accountability; and (c) leaders who fail to set clear expectations or follow through on

---

promises are culpable when things go wrong for their team. Connors and Smith conclude, "True accountability is not about punishment. It is not about taking revenge against someone who has failed to meet your expectations." Instead, it's about understanding accountability as a valuable and positive personal attribute in your team.

Instead of, "How did that happen?" Connors and Smith challenge leaders to ask, "How did I let that happen?"[38] Changing this one question has done more than almost anything else inside of Workfront to get people to speak the truth about our issues and obstacles.

UNDER PRESSURE, HOW DO WE RESPOND?

You'll recall at the beginning of this book I suggested that leaders choose their worldview: either assuming everyone is working with good intent or assuming everyone will try to shirk. Your world is most revealed by how you respond to your team when you are under pressure.

Dr. Rob McKenna is a good friend of mine and has a passion for studying leadership under pressure. This passion led him to work with the Boeing Company on a project where they followed the careers of 120 executives to explore factors and experiences that had the greatest impact on leadership development.[39]

Through many conversations with Rob, I interpret his definition of pressure to include any or all of these factors:

1. Driving change and dealing with the associated anxieties in an organization

2. Being on the edge of your performance or capability envelope in public
3. Having the possibility of a highly visible failure
4. Operating with outspoken disagreement of your decisions and/or direction
5. Assuming responsibility for the direction, success, and well-being of other people

If you lead modern work, by definition you do not always know exactly what you are doing. Your position is visible, factions within the organization are disagreeing with you, and many are dependent upon you for their livelihood. According to Dr. Rob, you are under pressure. So, when you are reviewing work and one of your folks pulls you aside and unloads a major mistake on you, what is your reaction to this person? If you are like me, your antenna tingles, looking for every bit and piece of data about the situation, and your brain starts formulating options. You are then likely to lay out to your team, in a high degree of detail, exactly what must get done to recover from the mistake or missed assignment. It is easy under pressure to become intensely concerned with *what they are doing.*

Early in my career at IBM, there was a legend of a promising young executive at the company in the 1960s. He had just led IBM into a risky venture that lost the company $10 million. When Tom Watson Sr., the founder and CEO of IBM, called the executive into his office, the executive arrived with his resignation letter already written. According to the legend, Watson retorted, "You cannot be serious, we have just spent $10 million dollars educating you!" If there is truth to the legend, Tom Watson was clearly focused on who this executive *was becoming,* not *what he was doing.*

We do need to get stuff done, so you cannot solely focus on who your team members are becoming. Instead, think of your situation as a numerical scale going from -10 to +10. The '-10' end-point is fully concerned with what they are doing and not concerned at all about who they are becoming. The '+10' end-point is fully concerned with who they are becoming and not concerned at all about what they are doing. In the highest-pressure moments, we want to lean into a style of coaching versus inspection, and to do so we merely need to spend the majority of our time on the + side of the scale. We need to have the self-awareness to drag ourselves just barely into the positive side when under duress; it will speak volumes to our team. When people believe you care about who they are becoming, their work will have meaning, and through that meaning their passion will increase.

Where do you stand with your team? If you see momentum starting to slide on a project, what will your response be? To coach or to inspect?

DEFY YOUR BLAME INSTINCT

The problem is, neutral language isn't your instinct. You're going to have to work on it. Blame seems to be hardwired into the parts of our brain most closely associated with emotional reactions, according to one study at Duke University. We're quicker to "judge actions leading to negative consequences as being more intentional than those leading to positive ones."[40] We're more likely to hold people personally responsible for their failures than for their successes.

Let's give the final word to Cynthia Boon. Her career has taken her a long way from the police emergency call and dispatch team in Euless, Texas, in the mid-1990s. Yet, the lessons she learned back then have set the tone for her approach to team communication today. Curious. Neutral. Quickly establishing trust. A focus on clarity about what's happening and what needs to be fixed. And as for criticism and negative feedback, there's a time for everything: "As much as you want to point your finger and say, 'You didn't do what you said you were going do, and you didn't do it in the time that you said you were going do it,' how is that going to help the situation? Blame can wait."

I've felt it during my career; no doubt you've felt it too. Blame seems to land from a greater height than praise lifts you to. Everyone hears the thud of blame when it hits someone's desk; all too often, praise happens in private. You're a better leader than that. Whether your team's goals have reached escape velocity or whether they're grounded, you've got to start asking the right questions, adopt the right tone, and pick the topics and projects where you'll give momentum a boost.

Escape Velocity

Maintain momentum by focusing intently on the right work

As we learned in this chapter, there are certain skills every leader must master when striving to maintain their team's momentum. This worksheet includes two exercises that will help you:

- Relentlessly inspect and accomplish BNAs
- Differentiate projects that are grounded from those that have achieved escape velocity

ACTIVITY #1: BNA CARD STACK

Imagine gathering a stack of index cards, and writing one BNA on each card, with the relevant key initiative in the upper left and the milestone in the upper right. Imagine relentlessly flipping through the index cards, making sure each BNA gets done. If you're old school, you can take this advice literally, using actual index cards. Or you can use modern work management technology in the same fashion.

KEY INITIATIVE:	MILESTONE:
BNA:	

TIP: You can hand a BNA "card" to someone else—either literally or digitally—requesting that they return and report when the BNA is complete. When the BNA is done, throw the card away and move on to the next one in the stack, continually adding more when the stack gets low.

ACTIVITY #2: ESCAPE VELOCITY GRAPH

This subjective activity will help leaders determine which key initiatives need more of your time and attention. Start by writing your five KIs from Exercise #4 on the lines below.

KI-1. _____

KI-2. _____

KI-3. _____

KI-4. _____

KI-5. _____

Now plot each one on the grid (using the abbreviations KI-1, KI-2, etc.) based on how much effort has been expended and how much progress is being made.

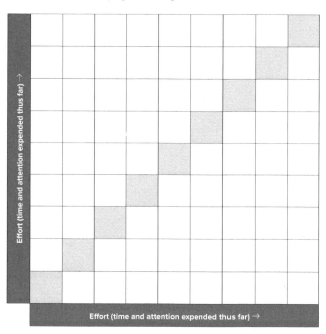

INTERPRETING THE GRAPH

If a key initiative is positioned above the gray diagonal line, it has achieved escape velocity; let it fly. If it's below the line, that bird is grounded; give it a boost.

7

Get People to Pay Attention

"What the eyes see and the ears hear, the mind believes."

—HARRY HOUDINI

The first weather satellite intended to chart the climate on another planet made its final approach to Mars on September 23, 1999.

"After traveling 416 million miles during the last nine months, Mars Climate Orbiter is now ready for its most dramatic moment, the orbit insertion burn," Dr. Sam Thurman, flight operations manager at NASA, told the world's media that day.[41]

And then … silence.

The orbiter vanished from mission control's scopes.

According to NASA engineer Richard Cook, "It was pretty clear that morning, within half an hour, that the spacecraft had more or less hit the top of the atmosphere and burned up."[42]

The investigation into the failure of the $125 million mission concluded that the orbiter had overshot its minimum viable orbit by just sixteen miles. Why did it overshoot? There had been a mix-up over imperial and metric units by different project teams — a communications glitch that played out in the orbiter's software. Welcome to another of Shootman's Laws of Leadership: in my experience, all projects will have at least three disasters and they won't be related to the technical tasks at hand. They will be rooted in communication. And it's usually not how you avoid the disaster that matters. It is how you handle them realizing that the disasters likely stem from miscommunication, vagueness, or failure to share vital details and decisions at the right time. What's certain is that if you don't work hard to get internal communication right, the price you will pay is loss of direction and momentum — and that's painful enough. For the Mars Climate Orbiter, the price paid was even higher: total mission failure and eternal fame as a mismanaged project.

Pretty much every business manual will tell you that great leaders are excellent communicators. In this chapter, we're going to break down what that means when you're trying to get modern work done. We'll focus on your two key problems: being heard and being understood. We'll explore what empathy really means with expert Brian Carroll. And we'll observe how master communicators — marketers Lee Odden and Jay Baer — handle internal communications in their own businesses.

Right from the start, keep in mind that the cost of poor leadership communications isn't abstract. This really counts. According to one study, "Companies that communicate effectively had a 47 percent higher return to shareholders over a five-year period (mid-2004 to mid-2009)."[43] Think about the timing of that study. It covers a period of economic boom to economic bust. The leaders who communicated effectively helped their companies prosper in good times and ride out the bad.

THE PROBLEM OF BEING HEARD

You probably think that being anointed a leader in a modern enterprise means everyone listens to you. Surprise! They don't. Or rather, they can't. You are one voice in a noisy workplace. By one estimate, Americans took in five times as much information every day in 2011 as they did in 1986 — the equivalent of 174 newspapers.[44]

The consequence of this barrage of content is that your team is making choices about what channels they'll pay attention to *first* based on what they feel works best for them. Take email as an example: You'll find an average of 199 unopened emails inside the mailbox of American workers. Split that down by generation, and you'll find that digital natives (a.k.a. millennials) are even more likely than their Generation X or baby boomer colleagues to leave messages unopened and unread.[45] Are younger employees more comfortable in leaving messages unread? Are they struggling to cope with the volume? Or maybe email is not their preferred content channel. The answer isn't clear and doesn't really matter. The point is: not every message is getting read — regardless of who is sending it. If you're thinking of typing your program's quarterly email update or a team briefing, step away from your keyboard now. You can't rely on "from the boss" being enough to make your message stick.

THE PROBLEM OF BEING UNDERSTOOD

Let's assume for a miraculous moment that your message gets read. The second problem is: Will they get your point? Welcome to Shootman's Transitive Law of Management Communication:

    A. All management actions are mysterious.

    B. All mysterious actions create conspiracy theories.

C. Therefore, all management actions create conspiracy theories.

It's a reworking of the transitive law of math created by the Victorian mathematician Augustus De Morgan, one of the forefathers of computer logic. In the workplace, Shootman's Law means that you need to accept that your actions and communications have the potential to create misunderstanding and conspiracy theories. People will always try to interpret what you do. They'll second-guess your reasoning, and they'll see patterns and connections that simply aren't there. According to a study at the UK's University of Kent, conspiracy theories are most prevalent when workers feel that they lack control, have little say over their duties, or experience workplace uncertainty — such as the appointment of new managers or a change in business direction.[46] You'll never cure a workplace of conspiracy theories, but you can strive for clarity about motive and action. If everyone understands what, when, how, and *why* things are happening, there's less room for speculation. Where conspiracy theories flourish, your efforts to make work meaningful will wither. You need to work relentlessly hard to be understood.

WANT PEOPLE TO PAY ATTENTION AND UNDERSTAND MORE? LISTEN BETTER

How do you slay this twin-headed beast: the struggle to be heard and the struggle to be understood? Follow the breadcrumbs through this book and you should have reached an important conclusion by now. You need to be close to your team. You need to understand *what they think* and *how they feel*. That's true whether you're crafting a vision to make work matter or engaging them in setting extraordinary goals. You need empathy.

If someone doesn't understand, it's on me

Never assume that what's clear to one person will be understood by someone else in the same way. That's the hard lesson I learned some years back when I was living in Italy and running development teams across seventeen countries. When I took a business trip to Thailand, a colleague picked me up at the airport and on the car trip to the hotel said, "Alex, I really don't get the strategy of the organization." Through the rest of the journey and all that night, I fumed. I'd explained this. I'd documented and presented this. What was the problem? When I woke the next morning, I realized that the failing was mine. This was a problem of explanation on my part. A leader is responsible for whether or not their team understands the plan, the strategy, and the vision. If someone doesn't get it, it's on you.

"Stop listening with the intent to reply, and start listening with the intent to understand," advises Brian Carroll, founder of Markempa and author of the best seller, *Lead Generation for the Complex Sale*.[47] Brian has studied the science of human behavior and has become one of America's best-known advocates for baking empathy into sales, marketing, and business operations. He believes most leaders make the mistake of "tuning in for eighteen seconds" to what other people are saying as they look for a shortcut to a decision. Instead, he advocates a change of mindset: Listen fully and be curious as a leader. Watch your team's nonverbal cues and micro-expressions. Read your people.

If they don't understand what you're saying — or don't like it — you'll read it in their faces and in their posture.

Repeat aloud what you've heard to ensure you've understood what's been said. "So, you mean this …" Follow this pattern in meetings and you'll not only gather the insight you need to understand your team better, but you'll also demonstrate a model of leadership behavior that others will start to follow. Your route to empathetic leadership will cultivate a more understanding, listening culture in your team.

Want people to pay attention and understand more? Start by listening better to them — and make it a habit. Dale Carnegie, author of *How to Win Friends and Influence People*, said famously that you'll make more friends in two months by being interested in other people than in two years of trying to get people interested in you. The leadership lesson is simple: "To be interesting, be interested."[48]

QUICK TEST: HIGH LISTENING, HIGH ADVOCACY = INFLUENCE

There's a simple test of whether you're listening, asserting, or influencing people. Plot what you're trying to say — and how you're trying to say it — against a 2x2 grid, with advocacy on one axis and inquiry on the other. If you rank high for inquiry but low for advocacy — you're listening. If you rank high for advocacy but low for listening — you're telling people what to do and asserting how things are. Great communicators understand the moment and therefore the communication need that goes with the moment. They pick the right quadrant to be in based upon the need of the team at the time. Sometimes you just need to observe.

LEE ODDEN'S LISTENING TIP: MONTHLY POLLS

When he's not consulting with clients, speaking at events around the world, or being cited for his marketing expertise by the *New York Times*, *Forbes*, or *Wall Street Journal*, you'll find Lee Odden at his agency, TopRank Marketing, in Minneapolis. Like Brian, Lee is convinced that listening is the first step to better internal communications. One of the tools he's introduced is a monthly staff poll to gauge employee sentiment. Lee asks his team these questions:Did you reach your goal last month?

- Did you get support to reach your goal?
- What were you most excited about in the past month?
- What were the biggest opportunities or challenges?

- What are you most excited about in your work in the coming month?
- What do you need help with?
- How likely are you to refer us as a potential employer to a friend?
- How likely are you to refer someone to hire us as an agency?

These are bellwether questions. The final question — "would you refer us?" — represent a classic digital marketing play. The poll plays to the same set of human sentiments we encounter on social media every day: we're always encouraged to react with a like, love, or dislike to the most important life events or most trivial of purchases. "In marketing, when you understand the goals, needs, and pain of your customers, you can use the insight that surfaces to architect more effective communication," says Lee. "There's an opportunity to do that with internal company communications too. Polls provide communication opportunities at the individual and organizational level, enabling us to surface opportunities on the spot, as well as compare response trends over time to our benchmarks."

If you're leading a workforce of thousands of people spread across a continent (or the globe), you need tools to gauge the mood of the whole team. Then you need to break that down into locations, business units, or even critical projects. Lee's regular polls are a good example of how you might do this at scale.

We're doing this at Workfront too. A Net Promoter Score (NPS)[49] survey within our company asks the same bellwether question: "Would you recommend Workfront to a friend?" The answers shape priorities in the company. We review the internal NPS score with the same cadence and care as the one we use with our customers.

Finally, if you're still in any doubt about the importance of empathy and listening to your team, flip the thinking around. If you don't care about how your team is feeling and you don't care about what worries them — or inspires them — how can you possibly find the words to make their work matter?

JAY BAER: HEIGHTENED FREQUENCY, REDUCED COMPLEXITY

Peek inside the offices of Convince & Convert and you'll see how one of America's best-known marketers, Jay Baer, handles communication with his team. Jay has become one of mainstream media's go-to commentators on marketing and branding, and his best-selling book *Youtility* has become a content marketing classic.[50] What Jay preaches to his clients about good communication, he puts into practice at his own business. He's created a program of "Webinines": short, focused video webinars lasting no more than nine minutes for his team. If nine minutes isn't enough, he'll run a sequence of separate Webinines covering a single subject in greater depth or spanning a range of topics. "I used to get voicemails, emails, and occasionally a letter — that was the list," says Jay. "Now you're bouncing back and forth between so many different channels all the time. You must communicate in smaller chunks because people's attention windows are reduced. There are some people who don't read beyond the first paragraph. It's a question of heightened frequency, reduced complexity."

Why does Jay favor video? Jay — like Brian — rightly argues that when you communicate face-to-face, the words you speak are supplemented by nonverbal cues. I know there will be more engagement inside of Workfront from a two-minute video I send than an 800-word email or blog post explaining the exact same thing. Even if I put "Read time no more than two minutes" as the subject line, people won't read to the end. A two-minute video *feels* less time-consuming than an 800-word read.

Now, don't read this as a hard rule that video is the best and only answer. Look around the digital ecosystem and you'll bump into Jay,

Lee, and Brian on pretty much every channel and in every format. You'll even find their thoughts conveyed best-selling books — and a book is the ultimate in long-form content! They are arch-experimenters, constantly trying different tools to share their messages via text, images, audio, and video. You should strive to be one too. Remember: heightened frequency, reduced complexity.

YOUR COMMUNICATION PLAYBOOK

If you want to be heard and understood — and lead modern work — you need to show genuine interest in others and share your messages generously rather than sparingly. And you need to accept that people are time-sliced and messages get fragmented.

Start by being a better listener: a more empathetic leader. Listen with the intent to understand rather than reply, as Brian counsels. This applies whether you're talking with coworkers, customers, or your financial stakeholders.

Plot how your communication fits when it comes to inquiry and advocacy to make sure your approach is right for the moment.

Scale your listening by applying techniques like Lee's monthly polls.

And when it comes to getting your message out, adopt Jay's "heightened frequency, reduced complexity" formula. Think of every channel you can use, not just the easiest one or what you feel most comfortable with. This isn't an either-or choice: you need to be omni-channel.

Be a story-listener as well as a storyteller. Be short, precise, and persuasive in your messaging. Speak often and don't neglect to talk about progress. We've all heard the phrase "walk the talk," but many times in managing modern work you must "talk the walk." People need to hear from you that they are making progress. Above all, recognize that conversations are more engaging than broadcasts. And remember, if they don't get it, it is still your responsibility.

Communication Playbook

Craft messages that are both heard *and* understood

As the leader, you own the communication around your key initiatives and extraordinary goals. But how do you determine the proper cadence and the best channels for keeping everyone engaged and in the loop? This exercise will help you accomplish the twin goals of "reduced complexity" and "heightened frequency."

STEP 1: DETERMINE WHAT YOU NEED TO COMMUNICATE

Pulling from previous exercises, fill out the table below. For each key initiative, record the last BNA that was accomplished as well as the next one in your stack. Why? So you can celebrate recent successes and maintain focus on what needs to happen next. This provides the foundation for WHAT you need to say: "Great job for completing X, let's rally the troops around Y."

WHAT ARE WE TRYING TO DO?			
Commander's intent			
HOW DO WE GET THERE?			
KEY INITIATIVE 1:		**KEY INITIATIVE 2:**	
EXTRAORDINARY GOAL:		**EXTRAORDINARY GOAL:**	
Last BNA:	Next BNA:	Last BNA:	Next BNA:
KEY INITIATIVE 3:		**KEY INITIATIVE 4:**	
EXTRAORDINARY GOAL:		**EXTRAORDINARY GOAL:**	
Last BNA:	Next BNA:	Last BNA:	Next BNA:

STEP 2: PLAN YOUR CHANNELS

Now you need to determine WHEN and HOW to share your message. Select a key initiative and write it below, placing checkmarks in the boxes to indicate both recent and upcoming communications around that KI. (Alternately, use a single table to map all key initiatives, writing "KI1," "KI2," "KI3," in the appropriate boxes.)

KI:

			CHANNELS					
			Email	Intranet	Meeting	Slack	Video	Live Video
FREQUENCY	RECENT COMMUNICATIONS	Last Month						
		Last Week						
	PLANNED COMMUNICATIONS	This Week						
		Next Week						
		This Month						

8

Out of Left Field

"Sometimes the system goes on the blink, and the whole thing it turns out wrong. ...You had a bad day."

—DANIEL POWTER, "BAD DAY"

"*Tell me your story.*" Providing this simple, open prompt in job interviews gives me more insight into a candidate's potential than anything they might tell me about the numbers they've hit or the projects and programs they've steered to a successful outcome. The best stories always show people on a journey. The story doesn't have to be an epic tale; an anecdote of how obstacles have been overcome and lessons have been learned will do. That's when I can see the caliber of leader the candidate will be since leadership skills are forged in the crucible of adversity. In fact, if a candidate proudly tells me, "I've never missed a number," I am not likely to hire them. I don't want to be the one who has to change their diaper, if you'll forgive the colorful metaphor! If you are going to master modern work, you *will* encounter adversity on the way. Things will never go exactly as you planned. But adversity, change — and yes, failure — are not your enemies. They are the opportunities to build the resilience to be the leader you want to be.

That's not to say change, adversity, and moments of failure aren't tough! We all have diaper days, and in this chapter I'll tell you about mine. The real question is: *how do you deal with it*? We'll explore how to be resilient in the face of nasty surprises, unanticipated mistakes, and failures you'll encounter during your leadership journey. You and your team will need reserves of determination, focus, and positivity at precisely the moments those qualities seem to desert you. Where do those reserves come from? Let's find out by looking at four ways you can build resilience when a problem comes "out of left field," which is American slang meaning "unexpectedly," "odd," or "strange." The phrase comes from baseball, referring to a play in which the ball is thrown from the left fielder to either home plate or first base, surprising the runner.

LEARNING RESILIENCE #1: LEAN TOWARDS THE OBSTACLES

My diaper day came in the spring of 2003. I was leading the sales team at BMC Software in Houston as we approached our March 31st fiscal year-end. Typically, almost 40 percent of what we sold during the entire year was closed in the last quarter. And we'd expect to close almost 80 percent of that in the last two weeks of the month. But with eleven days to go, the market vanished — thanks to geopolitics. The American-led coalition's invasion of Iraq began on March twentieth, prompting every major company and prospective client to shut down decision-making. Our final quarter and fiscal year fell off the table. We missed our numbers and our earnings guidance. Bitter disappointment doesn't come close to describing how I felt. But on the morning of April 1st, I found a handwritten note on my desk from my mentor and one of the company's vice presidents, Joseph "Chip" Nemesi. Chip wrote:

I stopped by this morning, but you were in the gym. Since you looked like you had just watched your puppy get run over last night, I wanted to check in on you this a.m. However, knowing you as well as I do, I know you have moved on to a new year and are walking with confidence and enthusiasm this morning. Your team will expect you to be mad and lack some confidence and conviction after a rough close, and as usual I know you will surprise them, and they will draw strength from your example.

Chip went on to write that he knew I'd never let "two or three accounts, a war, and an IT slump" affect my confidence or ability to lead. I've kept his note for fifteen years. It was a well-timed kick in the behind. Chip wrote things I did not yet feel. He described a course of action I had not yet imagined. With Chip's encouragement, I walked in the footsteps of the stranger he introduced me to. What did I learn from the experience? Through whatever successes, highs, and lows I've experienced since, I know that on the other side of failure is another chance to win again.

Accept that if you strive for the extraordinary, you will not always succeed. But also accept that you don't become great at getting extraordinary work done by avoiding risk, surprises, or mistakes. As legendary basketball coach John Wooden of UCLA once said, "If you're not making mistakes, then you're not doing anything. I'm positive that a doer makes mistakes."[51] The starting point for resilient leadership is to *see yourself on the other side of the surprise, mistake, or failure.* Embrace the obstacles; they are the only things that will reveal to you who you really are.

LEARNING RESILIENCE #2: OWN YOUR RESILIENCE

Not everyone has the good fortune to have a Chip Nemesi on hand to deliver an elegant motivational kick at just the right time. There are techniques leaders can use to build their own resilience — and tips they can pass on to their team about dealing with adversity when it strikes. Meet one of the most remarkable people I know, Debra Searle. Whatever "out of left field" surprises I have endured pale by comparison to Debra's story.

Debra is a successful entrepreneur, author, and television presenter — and she's been twice-honored by the Queen of England for her achievements in her native UK and beyond. She has a mental toolkit that served her well through one of the toughest tests imaginable. Adversity was her everyday companion for three and a half months on a solo feat of endurance: she rowed across 3,000 miles of ocean by herself in a boat built for two.

Debra's story starts in 2001 when she set off from the Spanish island of Tenerife with her then-husband Andrew on a transatlantic rowing challenge bound for Barbados. While Andrew was a top-level club oarsman, Debra was a novice who had never rowed on the open ocean before. The couple had prepped for their voyage on the quiet waters of the River Thames in London. But just fourteen days into their journey, Andrew was forced to drop out. Struck by a pathological fear of the open ocean — facing crippling panic attacks and blackouts — he was taken off the boat by a rescue yacht. Debra, aged twenty-seven at the time, faced a choice: abandon the challenge or continue alone. She carried on. Debra battled with fierce ocean currents and Atlantic storms that could wipe out a day's progress in a matter of hours. Every process on the boat was designed for two people, not one. And, throughout it all, Debra battled with nagging self-doubt. Could she finish what she started? The challenge took her more than twice the time originally planned. But when she arrived in Barbados, Debra made headlines around the world. How did she keep going? Debra says it was a matter of "mindset, not magic." So, what was in her mental toolkit?

1. Channel your alter ego

Debra, five feet, two inches tall, imagined herself as Xena: Warrior Princess during the voyage — an Amazonian archetype of female strength and courage from a 1990s TV show. "Imagining your alter ego helps you prepare for the work ahead," she says. "I don't know how many times I've imagined that I'm the British entrepreneur Richard Branson before a business meeting or negotiation." We all have heroes. Some come from fiction or history, like Debra's. I find my inspiration in everyday heroes, such as a colleague at Workfront who faces every day with determination and optimism despite a Stage 4 cancer diagnosis. When I look at what he does and continues to do, I'm inspired. What model of courage or conviction would you channel in a moment of crisis?

2. Find memory songs

"I'm not naturally the kind of person who leaps out of bed full of the joys of spring; sometimes I need a little help," she says. Turning on music and playlists that stirred positive thoughts and memories helped Debra stick to her challenge in her darkest hours. When you're struggling for motivation or feeling dragged down by the weight of the problems that you face, what track would lift your spirits? My go-to is "Don't Look Back" by Boston. You'll hear it whenever I take the stage at a Workfront conference: *"Don't look back, a new day is breaking, it's been too long since I felt this way. I don't mind where I get taken, the road is calling and today is the day."*

3. Have a contagious belief

"I felt I was the luckiest person alive on so many of the days I was out there," Debra says. She felt good fortune to be engaged in such an adventure! And positive belief and self-belief is contagious — if you're in an office rather than alone in a boat on the open ocean, your belief will be passed on to those around you. Think about Chip's letter. He reminded me that my attitude would help to inspire those around me. It's about seeing a roadblock in proper perspective and understanding that overcoming obstacles is part of every great story.

4. Shift out of your comfort zone to innovate

"I was innovating like you wouldn't believe — the comfort zone shifted eventually to where it needed to be," Debra says as she describes trying to manage a boat designed for two. Today, she applies the same thinking to her businesses. What lies outside the organization's comfort zone that could be a route to innovation?

5. Play the arrival scene

"It was never really a solo effort — without my family and supporters I never would have made it," Debra says. She describes imagining achieving her goal: arriving at Port St. Charles in Barbados at the end of her journey and being reunited with her family and friends. "Playing the arrival scene" — visualizing her goal — kept her motivated at the toughest moments of the challenge. Imagine getting the call that you've won a new contract. Imagine seeing coworkers achieve more than ever before — hitting an Extraordinary Goal. Tell yourself what that will feel like. This takes us right back to the beginning of the book and the work you've done at the start of your leadership journey. Your arrival scene is the vision you create for your team.

6. Use words wisely

Debra describes how receiving texts of encouragement from strangers via satellite phone made her think carefully about the power of words, which are free and in never-ending supply! Choose those words wisely; be selective about the words you say to yourself. And never gripe or complain: you're only enabling coworkers to do the same. Chip's words were so powerful I've shared them — and the story behind them — with every leader I've ever worked with.

7. Choose your attitude

"This is the one thing I had a choice about. Every day I made an attitude choice: I said it out loud. It had to be a positive attitude — negative attitudes were banned on the boat," Debra says. The choice you make about your own attitude is a key step in building your resilience.

Debra's mental toolkit is about more than positivity; it's about choosing your outlook when everything feels out of control. It's about the need to step back from the intense stress of the moment to take a longer view. Try Debra's toolkit whenever you're charting unfamiliar territory or facing adversity. Maybe your challenge will be like the vanishing market I faced in 2003. Perhaps it's a project that's been grounded by an unexpected problem — overrunning costs or shifting scope. These attitude tools won't solve the problems you're facing, but they'll put you in a healthier frame of mind to try to determine the best next action.

LEARNING RESILIENCE #3: KEEP COMMUNICATING

The Bontrager Flare R bicycle taillight has become one of Trek's signature products — a best seller. Visible at two kilometers in daylight — when 80 percent of bike accidents happen — it's a shining symbol of the company's commitment to both safety and quality.[52] But its birth was a testing time. The engineering team lived through three years of high passion and unexpected obstacles. As Trek's Engineering Project Manager Sean Pederson recalls, the Flare R was a new product line with new technology, and pretty much everyone on the project was new to the team. There was an ambition to export the sensor-rich tail-light to new markets around the world. "It was a constant emotional battle," says Sean. "I had people stopping by my desk, seemingly on the hour, to voice their personal concerns over what was being done. I have passionate engineers, designers. I have passionate people who work in quality and warranty. I have passionate marketing team members. But their vision for the product was not aligning."

Ironically, the number one factor behind their passion was bureaucracy — unexpected regulations, testing requirements, costs, and timeframes to certify the product. For example, a single product test to certify for the Chinese market took more than three months — a delay that had not been anticipated or planned for. How did Sean — at the heart of this storm — see the project to a successful conclusion? "I realized that just listening to people's concerns and giving them, if nothing else, a sounding board in me, helped to ease their concerns," he says. "There are some things you can control; there are some things you cannot. But if I hadn't been through the experience, I wouldn't know how to handle probably 80 percent of the challenges that are thrown at me today." Leadership skills are forged by the challenges you overcome. And there's a practical tip. Keep talking. Keep listening. Just like Sean, be the level head when everyone else around is losing theirs. That's what resilience looks like.

LEARNING RESILIENCE #4: ACCEPT THAT YOU CAN'T WIN IF YOU DON'T RISK LOSING

Back in the 1960s, Green Bay Packers coach Vince Lombardi led his team to five NFL Championships in seven years — including three back-to-back victories. The NFL Super Bowl trophy is named in his honor. He once quipped, "Show me a good loser and I'll show you a loser." Lombardi's words are considered gospel in NFL circles. But too often words like this create the wrong reaction; we read it as, "Show me someone who loses, and I'll show you a loser." Lombardi's record was 105-35-6; 25 percent of the time he stepped on the field he lost; 28 percent of the time he did not win. He never said "don't lose"; that's not what he meant. He wanted passion and commitment. And he wanted his players to hate losing. I hate to lose too. But I've learned that I won't win all the time, however hard I strive for success. To succeed, you must face the risk of failure and be resilient to whatever comes out of left field. What keeps me going in tough times is the knowledge that success tomorrow lives on the other side of today's failure. There's always another chance to win.

THE BEST KIND OF MISTAKE TO LEARN FROM IS SOMEONE ELSE'S

Thus far, we've looked for resilience on the other side of failure. But there's an important caveat to this focus on the future. Before you speed ahead, reflect on what went wrong — and what was working — when that unexpected challenge came out of left field. Or, as veteran project manager Eric Lucas quips, "When you're standing in the swamp with alligators all around, don't discard everything that's gone right." Eric is PMO manager at Crowley Maritime Corporation, a family-owned international logistics and transportation business in Florida. He's well placed to give advice. Through a twenty-eight-year-career, he has managed about 1,000 projects. Do the math: that's an average of thirty-six projects per year — some large, some small program implementations — a run-rate that would make most managers tremble.

"I've never had one where *everything* goes wrong," says Eric, "I've had them where it *feels* like everything's going wrong."

Eric signals a crucial distinction. How you feel is all about resilience and looking forward. But learning lessons is about establishing hard facts and looking back. So take the time to reflect on the good and the bad after a point of failure. Hold a project debrief.

Every organization does that, right? Well, that's not what former US Navy SEAL Commander Mark McGinnis sees when he visits businesses these days. In nine out of ten cases, he sees an absence of "Corporate Battle Rhythm" — a full cycle of planning, briefing, execution, and debriefing on every project. He's not talking about an end-of-year or half-year review but routine debriefing about work in progress as milestones are reached and key initiatives completed. Following that rhythm is what distinguishes truly elite teams from merely good teams. According to Mark:

> *After a mission, we immediately come together in a hallowed environment where there's no rank, no blame, no privilege, no seniority, and we sit down and talk unemotionally about the successes and failures of the mission. It's important to capture both — the successes because we want to continue to do things that are working and the failures because we can't afford to make the same mistake twice. If we repeat mistakes in my world it has catastrophic results.*

The outcome of a SEAL team's debrief isn't kept within the mission squad. The lessons are open to every SEAL, from the top to bottom rank. "I'm accelerating everyone's experience, whether they're going out and doing operations or not," says Mark. "And we don't do that in the corporate world." It's time we did. After all, when dealing with the unexpected, the best kind of mistake to learn from is someone else's.

Mental Toolkit

Make a plan to deal with the unexpected

We have very little control over the external variables that make plans go awry—geopolitics, market conditions, a partner's pathological fear of the open ocean. Inspired by Debra Searle, who rowed solo across the Atlantic in a boat built for two, this exercise will help you build resilience in the face of adversity.

BUILD YOUR MENTAL TOOLKIT

Resilience, according to Debra, is all about "mindset not magic." Your resilience toolkit will consist of four things to decide in advance, and three practices to enact in the midst of an unexpected storm.

BEFORE YOU SET SAIL	**TOOL 1: ALTER EGO** Someone you channel when you need a dose of courage.	**EXAMPLE** Debra calls upon her inner Xena: Warrior Princess—or business magnate Richard Branson.	Whose example is a source of strength to you?
	TOOL 2: MEMORY SONGS A song, album, or playlist you can play (audibly or mentally) during challenging times.	**EXAMPLE** I play *Don't Look Back* by Boston whenever I take the stage at a Workfront Conference.	What is your fight song?
	TOOL 3: CONTAGIOUS BELIEF A positive belief or personal motto you can call upon when times get tough.	**EXAMPLE** "I felt I was the luckiest person alive on so many of the days I was out there," says Debra.	What is your contagious belief?
	TOOL 4: DISCOMFORT ZONE The practice of voluntarily pushing yourself beyond your comfort zone, so you'll feel more "comfortable" there when unexpected challenges arise.	**EXAMPLE** I recently rappelled down the side of Workfront's 5-story office building, despite an intense fear of heights.	How are you expanding your comfort zone today?
IN THE MIDST OF A STORM	**TOOL 5: ARRIVAL SCENE** What it looks like, feels like, and sounds like when you arrive safely on the other side of this challenge.	**EXAMPLE:** Debra continually envisioned arriving safely in Barbados, being reunited with family and friends.	What does your arrival scene look like?
	TOOL 6: WORDS OF ENCOURAGEMENT Supportive thoughts you would offer to someone else in your situation.	**EXAMPLE:** I often draw on Chip Nemesi's words: "I know you will surprise them, and they will draw strength from your example."	What can you say to yourself and others to build resilience?
	TOOL 7: ATTITUDE CHOICE The outlook you choose when everything feels out of control.	**EXAMPLE:** Says Debra: "Every day I made an attitude choice: I said it out loud. It had to be a positive attitude— negative attitudes were banned on the boat."	What is your attitude today?

DONE *right*

THREE NIGHTMARES

The anticipation of a terrible event is always worse than the event itself. To help build up your immunity to unexpected challenges, write three nightmare scenarios and then apply the last three tools to them for practice.

TIP: You can pull some of the nightmare scenarios you brainstormed on the milestone level in Exercise #5, or invent new ones.

NIGHTMARE #1:

Scenario: _____

Arrival Scene: _____

Words of Encouragement: _____

Attitude Choice: _____

NIGHTMARE #2:

Scenario: _____

Arrival Scene: _____

Words of Encouragement: _____

Attitude Choice: _____

NIGHTMARE #3:

Scenario: _____

Arrival Scene: _____

Words of Encouragement: _____

Attitude Choice: _____

9

Measuring Modern Work

*"There are two possible outcomes: if the result confirms the
hypothesis, then you've made a measurement. If the result is
contrary to the hypothesis, then you've made a discovery."*

—ENRICO FERMI

History doesn't record the crowd's reaction when a twenty-five-
year-old engineer stepped onto the court at the first US National
Tennis Championship in 1881. He was carrying a racket of his own,
carefully researched and designed, with an unusual spoon-shaped
head that deviated from the traditional lopsided paddles used at the
time. Was the crowd amused at the spectacle as he walked out to
play? Were they shocked at the sight of such an odd racket? Whatever
skepticism might have been in the air that summer, the young engineer became one half of the winning men's doubles pair in the forerun-
ner tournament of the US Open. Yet, despite making sporting history,
that's not what he's remembered for nearly a century and a half later.
Visit his grave in Bala Cynwyd, Pennsylvania, and you'll read the epi-
taph: "Fredrick Winslow Taylor: The Father of Scientific Management."

Taylor's racket design hints at the guiding philosophy of his life. He believed the application of scientific principles was the route to efficient and improved performance in any field, from the tennis court to the factories of late nineteenth and early twentieth- century America. At the Pennsylvania steel plants where he worked, he stalked with a stopwatch — precisely recording the speed and volume of production. Then he designed new, more efficient working methods. After watching men trying to move tons of iron ore with the same spade as men moving piles of ash, he designed a series of new shovels tailored for each task.[53] His 1911 book, *The Principles of Scientific Management*, has been described as the world's first business best seller.[54] He won Henry Ford's admiration and influenced Vladimir Lenin's thinking about Soviet production. In the organizations that adopted Taylor's methods, "Most jobs needed less of everything — less brains, less muscle, less independence." He helped to define a working world where "everything clacked and whirred faster."[55]

So, will Taylor's methods reign in the world of modern work? Not exactly. Taylor famously wrote, "In the past the man has been first; in the future the machine must be first."[56] In this chapter, I'll show you that modern work is about the person *and* the machine. And in this new world, we need new metrics.

Here's why. You can see Taylor's influence in the key operating metrics used by various industries today: from Revenue Seat Miles in airlines to Room Occupancy in hotels to Average Revenue per User in the wireless industry. Look back to the story of George Biel in Chapter 4, and you'll see a dash of Taylorism in George's working recipe for Houston's Restaurants. This taste for data science has influenced public policy and government too. We have measures such as the Consumer Price Index, Consumer Confidence Index, and the Purchasing Manager's Index. The belief in measurement born with Taylor is now part of our private lives — the "Quantified Self" — where we're recording Body

Mass Index, Basic Metabolic Rate, cholesterol levels, and even the number of steps we take in a day.[57] The question is: Do key operating metrics that shaped the early twentieth century industrial era still fit today's digital, social, and mobile workforce? Do they fit knowledge work as well as they suited the exercise of strength and sweat?

The short answer is no. Let's be honest, they didn't really fit the final quarter of the twentieth century either. For example, look at the history of the US car industry. In the 1970s and 1980s, the big American automakers started to lose global and domestic market share to their Japanese competitors. While US production lines were still in the thrall of Taylorism, Japanese automakers adopted *"quality"* as their byword. As a result, seven of the top ten best-selling cars and trucks in the US today are Japanese.[58] Consistent quality beat consistent efficiency of production.

Taylorism, as the American car industry found to its cost, was an incomplete answer to running a successful business in the late twentieth century. And the more we turn repetitive manual work over to machines in the twenty-first century, the more we will value creativity, quality, and innovation in our human workforce. In short, we are going to prize the attributes that Taylor would have struggled to measure. Leaders will look at their team and wonder: How creative have you been? How much empathy have you shown to colleagues in need of motivation? How much charm have you expended to turn a cold lead into a hot sales prospect? How innovative are you? We may not be able to measure these elements, but that does not remove the responsibility to measure the overall work environment to determine if you've given your teams and your organization the best chance to succeed. To adapt to today's evolving markets, masters of modern work will need to focus on *work performance indicators (WPIs).*

WORK PERFORMANCE INDICATORS

More than 467 million hours — or 50,000 years — of work have been executed in Workfront's modern work management application. And after watching more than 3,000 customers execute all this work, we have identified five work performance indicators that should be applied in every organization. The WPIs retain the spirit of Taylorism but aim to bring his philosophy into the twenty-first century and meld the person and the system. Here's our starting point: to bring the benefits of Taylorism to the world of modern work. We need to measure mix, capacity, velocity, quality, and engagement.

Mix: What are you working on?

The first WPI helps leaders gauge what kind of work is being done across the business. The team's time and energy must be devoted to productive and positive activity that will take the organization closer to its goals. This WPI breaks down activity into two categories:

1. Running the organization
2. Changing the organization: creating something new

You want to measure the proportion of work allocated to *run* versus *change/create*. This will show you how much effort is being allocated to what matters. If you're pushing to change the business, you should expect to see an increased proportion of work in the *change* bucket. The Mix WPI will help you understand, at an organizational level, if your strategy has any real work allocation applied to it or not.

Capacity: How do you know if the work can get done?

The second WPI is capacity. This WPI is both a measure of the total capacity available and the capacity utilization of your enterprise. This helps you identify how much more work your organization can handle. The Capacity WPI is a modern-era update of a familiar Taylor metric. In the industrial age, Taylor's followers wanted to measure manufacturing capacity and utilization. For much of the last fifty years, the average manufacturing capacity utilization averaged 80 percent.[59] But separate studies by Workfront and McKinsey have found that modern worker utilization is less than 40 percent. That represents more than $3 trillion of wasted human capital investment each year.[60] Yes, *trillion*. If you ran a manufacturing company at 40 percent of capacity, you would be fired or out of business. With modern work management tools, we can do much better than that. Leaders of knowledge-driven businesses can use the Capacity WPI to determine how much more their organization can do.

Velocity: How fast are you working?

With the third WPI, velocity, you measure the total work cycle time — how long it takes to complete a piece of work — and how frequently work is done in the time originally committed (work-to-commit ratio). In other words, the Velocity WPI tells you how long it's taking your organization to get things done. Ultimately, this metric is about the speed of fulfillment. The market today values choice and immediacy. We live in an "I want what I want when I want it" culture. E-stores with expedited delivery services like Amazon Prime have conditioned us to believe, "I can get it tomorrow." We're becoming accustomed to being impatient. For example, surveys done by Akamai and Gomez. com have found that nearly half of web users expect a site to load in two seconds or less. And those users will tend to abandon a site that isn't loaded within three seconds.[61] To win in the modern world of work, you need to get your offer to market fast — and faster than anyone else. The Velocity WPI will help flag if work is taking too long. After all, in a modern work environment, speed kills.

Quality: Making sure you've got the best work

Traditional quality assurance systems measure the quality of the final output. They answer an obvious question: is this product good enough to put in front of customers? But the new Quality WPI measures something different: the perception of work quality *within* the organization. Is the person who commissioned a piece of work from a coworker, team, or department happy with the quality of work they've done? This could be as simple as a one-to-five scale or bubble rating trended over time, *"To what degree did the work match your original expectations?"* For example, both TripAdvisor and Amazon have influenced millions of consumer decisions based on their simple bubble and star ratings. These simple ratings are crowd-sourced proof points of quality. Tracking this WPI over time will help you understand if teams are producing work that meets the needs of the stakeholders they serve.

Engagement: Is there pride in the quality of work?

The fifth and final WPI is engagement. You're going to track your team's sense of pride in the work they accomplish. As we learned back in Chapter 1, people do their best work when they understand their role, believe their role matters, and are proud of the work they do. The engine of modern work is a human being, and the fuel of that engine is motivation. You would never think of operating a vehicle without a gauge to tell you when fuel is running low. The Engagement WPI flags when commitment and belief in the task, project, team, or organization is waning — and you need to act to revive that belief and commitment. Recall that in Chapter 7, Lee Odden at TopRank described monthly polls to help listen better to employees and track changes in their sentiment at work over time. The Engagement WPI would be measured by asking the simple questions, *"Did you understand what was expected of you? Did the work you were assigned make a difference to the organization? Did you do great work?"*

As the neuroscientist Antonio Damasio said, "We are not think-ing machines that feel, rather we are feeling machines that think."[62] Modern work is not stamped out by a machine press; modern work is thought out by Natasha, Sam, or Miguel or maybe all three of them working together. You need to track how engaged they are over time.

Can you measure the unmeasurable?

How do you find a needle in a haystack?

Bring a giant magnet — or set it on fire, then look when it's cooled down.

Those were two of the suggested answers to one of Google's infamously difficult interview questions.[63] The questions are a quick test of mental agility — of creativity at a moment of stress. A candidate for a program manager's job at Microsoft was once asked, "How would you design an airport?" — not because airport design was part of the job, but as a way of test-ing breadth of thinking and the candidate's approach to problem-solving.[64]

These types of interview questions echo the famous Torrance Test of Creative Thinking — a test carried out in 1972 with 400 children in a Minneapolis elementary school. Researcher Ellis Paul Torrance looked for evi-dence of divergent thinking: how many different ideas, across different categories, and in how much detail could children come up with in response to the same stimuli or question? Torrance looked at the statistical rarity of the answers to arrive at a measure of original-ity. When researchers caught up with the original 1972 cohort as adults, they found a correlation between the original creativity scores and what those adults were doing in their professional lives. There was a stronger correlation between those creativity scores and adult outcomes than their childhood IQ. Being creative isn't just about being academically smart.[65] Google and Microsoft are right. Try to gauge creativity at the point of hiring someone to join your team!

WHAT ABOUT COST?

Why isn't cost one of our twenty-first century WPIs? Sure, cost and expenditure are important. But many a fool has broken their pick on trying to execute enterprise-wide activity-based costing.[66] There are either too many or too few identified activities and cost drivers, which leads to infinite debates over cost-allocation methodologies. Ideally, cost data should always be integrated into modern work management systems. But be careful about the impact of this data on decision-making. It tends to give poor results and requires multiple manipulations to get an answer.

Our FIVE WPIs are most valuable when combined. You will gain the greatest insights from how the WPIs trend and the picture they paint if assessed together. Let's say you have a great mix ratio, available capacity, slow velocity, great quality, and high engagement. This tells you your team can do better work, but processes might be getting in your way.

Perhaps instead you have a bad mix, not much available capacity, good velocity, high quality, and low engagement. You might have some of your best resources focused on the wrong work and by reallocating them you can get breakout accomplishments. One simple dashboard with up and down arrows on the FIVE WPIs can tell you most anything you need to know to steer your organization. Think of these WPIs as pulling you out of the engine room and up on onto the bridge of a battleship; or better yet, the USS *Enterprise*. "Course heading, Captain?" — "Second star to the right, and straight on 'til morning."

HOW THE FIVE WPIs MIGHT EVOLVE

A final thought: Let's not make the mistake of thinking these five WPIs are good for the rest of this century. They are certain to change as technology, markets, and society changes.

How might they evolve? James Veall, senior vice president at Viacom, the multinational media corporation behind Paramount, MTV, Nickelodeon, and Comedy Central, suggests "relationships" as a future performance measure. James is talking about working relationships in a future when human performance is augmented by artificial intelligence (AI). You won't be collaborating only with humans but also with AI assistants. You can already see the early iterations in the form of Apple's Siri, Microsoft's Cortana, or Google's range of voice-activated tools. You can see the emerging future in today's chatbots and virtual diary assistants. As machine learning develops, these tools are only going to get more sophisticated. James predicts that the traditional efficiency metrics will become "meaningless." "What you'll need to measure is the quality of relationships," James says. "You're measuring how well the human is interacting with the machine. And, as a leader, you're measuring how well you influence the humans who are working around the machine."

Tom Amies-Cull, chief operating officer of UK Media Brands for Dentsu Aegis Network — a global family of marketing and communications businesses — suggests another way the WPIs might evolve.

Tom says he thrives at work through a "perpetual sense of growing and learning" and working with people who want to learn and grow too. This echoes Professor Teresa Amabile's thoughts about progress from Chapter 1. Could one of the success measures of future organizations be the velocity and impact of collective learning? This would shift the emphasis of our *run* and *change/create* equation firmly towards *change/create*. If AI is helping run the organization and all organizations are being equally well run, what will differentiate winning organizations from struggling ones? The answer is likely to be rate of transformation, innovation, and change. You won't be able to survive by being a well-run operation alone. If that turns out to be true, we are indeed rebooting what Frederick Winslow Taylor did a century ago: We're making a virtue of close study and learning as the route to sustainable, improved performance. And we will have done that by measuring the (supposedly) unmeasurable.

But for right now, these five WPIs — mix, capacity, velocity, quality, and engagement — will help you get everything in your organization clacking and whirring faster. Deploy them and adapt them to suit your marketplace and business conditions. You'll get a clearer view of what's happening inside your organization, what you need to fix, and where you're winning already. Frederick Winslow Taylor would approve.

Work Performance Indicators

Improve your visibility with these five WPIs

There are five work performance indicators (WPIs) that, when combined, can give you a clearer view of what's happening inside your organization, revealing what you need to fix and where you're winning already.

PART 1: EVALUATE YOUR ORGANIZATION

Let's start with a quick, subjective evaluation to see where your organization stands today.

WORK PERFORMANCE INDICATOR (WPI)	CIRCLE ONE
MIX: Does the proportion of work allocated to RUN vs CHANGE/CREATE match your goals for the business?	⬆ ⬇
CAPACITY: Does your organization have adequate bandwidth and resources?	⬆ ⬇
VELOCITY: How frequently is work done in the time originally committed?	⬆ ⬇
QUALITY: Are your team members satisfied with the quality of the work they're producing?	⬆ ⬇
ENGAGEMENT: Do your team members understand their roles, believe they matter, and feel pride in the work?	⬆ ⬇

Look at your particular combination of upward and downward arrows, and compare it to the examples on the facing page. Fill in the blanks below with an appropriate adjective for each WPI (weak, strong, poor, excellent, etc.). Then write your own interpretation of the results, in the style of the assessments at right.

We have: _____ **Mix,** _____ **Capacity,** _____ **Velocity,**

_____ **Quality, and** _____ **Engagement.**

What it means: _____

_____

PART 2: INTERPRET THE RESULTS

The following examples will help you understand how the five WPIs work together to help you see where you need to focus more time and attention.

EXAMPLE #1: Let's say you have bad mix, low capacity, good velocity, high quality, and low engagement.

WHAT IT MEANS: You have your best resources focused on the wrong work.

M	⬇
C	⬇
V	⬆
Q	⬆
E	⬇

EXAMPLE #2: You might also have great mix, available capacity, slow velocity, great quality and high engagement.

WHAT IT MEANS: Your team is capable of producing better work, but processes are getting in your way.

M	⬆
C	⬆
V	⬇
Q	⬆
E	⬆

EXAMPLE #3: Or you could have a bad mix, great capacity, poor velocity, excellent quality, but poor engagement.

WHAT IT MEANS: You need to work on your vision, and align your available talent and resources toward unified goals that are communicated clearly at all levels of the organization.

M	⬇
C	⬆
V	⬇
Q	⬆
E	⬇

PART 3: IDENTIFY AND COMMUNICATE YOUR TOP TWO WPIs

Determine from the results above the **one** or **two** WPIs that offer the greatest opportunity for improvement, and use them to complete the following script. You now have the ability to make any executive's jaw drop as you illustrate the business impact of effectively measuring modern work.

Our two greatest opportunities to improve the way we work are in the areas of:

_____ and _____
(WPI)   (WPI)

These improvements will have the following impact on the organization:

_____
(Relate this response to your Vision Statement from Exercise #1.)

We'll accomplish these improvements by enacting these key initiatives:

KI-1: _____

KI-2: _____

KI-3: _____
(Refer back to Exercise #4 for help crafting your key initiatives.)

10

The Future of Work ... Now

"The future ain't what it used to be."

—YOGI BERRA

Where in the world is Jen Gilligan? If I'd asked that question back in 2017, the answer would have been easy. Jen was in London at the *Daily Telegraph,* one of Britain's biggest newspapers, where she managed technical projects. But the last I heard from her, twenty-eight-year-old Jen was heading for India, then the Himalayas. By now, she might have switched continents and be trekking through the Brazilian rainforests. Just as her career was taking off, she decided to leave work behind for a while. Jen took off from London's Heathrow Airport in search of adventure.

Jen's decision to take an early career break is one of the signature stories of her generation: millennials in search of a meaningful life. But she also hopes the world of work will look a little different when she returns — whenever that may be. Jen isn't expecting a sudden switch to AI-driven bots, virtual assistants, and voice control technology. Nor is she imagining the kind of automated office nirvana that some in Silicon Valley dream of. Instead, she hopes for simple changes to how tomorrow's leaders think about what they do and why they do it. First, Jen hopes they'll work harder to clarify how they structure, track, and complete tasks. "If everyone knows what needs to be done and how best to do it, they'll be able to think more clearly and be more creative," says Jen. Don't bolt on new tech to old processes, she suggests, until you've really figured out how you do what you do. Her second hope is for less hierarchical communication. Let good ideas flower, wherever they have taken root.

Jen's hopes for the future of work echo the book's key themes:

1. Work needs to matter (Chapter 1).
2. The path needs to be clear; everyone needs to buy in to the journey (Chapters 3, 4, and 5).
3. The way leaders marshal their team must be more collaborative and engaging than in the past (Chapters 3, 6, and 7).
4. Everyone is creative; the answer to any problem is likely already in the room (Chapters 1, 2, 3, and 8).

This book was written with talented folks like Jen in mind. They are tomorrow's leaders, and I've been fortunate to meet many of them. In their presence I am bullish about the future of work and, frankly, the future in general. Leadership is going to get a lot better, since their values and priorities are ultimately going to have the greatest impact on the future of work.

In this final chapter, we'll look at the themes we've explored so far in the context of demographic changes and technological advances that continue to reshape the workplace.

DEMOGRAPHICS

Let's start with the demographic forces that are changing business culture — for the better. Jen's generation, the millennial generation (born from 1981 to 1996), is better educated than its predecessors. Millennial women are four times as likely as their grandmothers to have a college education; millennial men twice as likely as their grandfathers.[67] That doesn't mean they are innately smarter. It means they've been taught through to their early twenties to be intellectually curious and to challenge conventional wisdom. This is the generation that wonders, "Why?"

Thanks to the internet and the advent of consumer digital technology, they've grown up connected to the world in a way no preceding generation has been. They're more likely to use the internet, own a smartphone, use social media, and experiment with emerging digital platforms and mobile technologies than even their older brothers and sisters in Generation X. This is a generation that expects to constantly communicate and work anywhere. As the *Washington Post* put it, "for digital nomads, work is where the laptop is."[68]

And by every measure, the millennial generation bucks conformity in the workplace more than ever before. This generation will kick against being worker drones — where everyone looks the same, does the same, thinks the same.[69]

The impact of millennials on workplace culture affects their older coworkers. If our digitally nomadic millennials want flexibility at work, won't others want it? If millennials want fluid, non-hierarchical communication, won't that change how meetings work and coworkers interact? I believe it will. After all, grandparents use Facebook even if it was first built for college students.[70] The digital habits and cultural preferences of one generation influence the outlook and habits of others if they can see benefits of working in the same way. James Veall, senior vice president at Viacom, predicts that the tail end of the baby boomer generation (born 1946 to 1964) won't retire in the same way as those who came before them. "I think there will be this big shift towards temporary work contracts, and people working more of a portfolio type career as they get older," says James. "They'll do a couple of days here, a couple days there, particularly people that have been in the knowledge workspace. You're going to see a reasonably high percentage of workers moving through their careers on looser employment contracts, staying around for longer."

You are going to have a multi-generational workforce. The older workers will adopt the habits and characteristics of their younger coworkers — as far as it suits their needs. They too will be nomadic, seek flexibility, and seek clarity of intent — just as Jen Gilligan described. You will fail to successfully manage the workplace of the future if you cannot give meaning to work and provide mechanisms to organize, manage, and complete work so that your wanderlust workforce can be proud of what they do.

WORKPLACE TECHNOLOGY

Technology has evolved so rapidly since the World Wide Web went live in 1991 that old organizational hierarchies are increasingly redundant — it's just nobody told most businesses that's the case.[71] Data moves faster and in far more abundant quantities than at any other point in human history (see Eric Schmidt, Chapter 6). The idea that someone sitting at the top of a multi-layered hierarchy can process all the data they need to make good decisions is nonsense. Eddie Obeng, author, business founder, TED speaker, and professor of entrepreneurship at the UK's Henley Business School, explains it like this:[72]

If you're running an organization with a hierarchy and top team, when they sit around the boardroom table, there is a maximum speed at which you can get information into that group to make a decision — about ten megabits per second. In the old world, you could get an idea to a boss, they could make a decision, and pass it down. Now information is moving at a thousand times that speed. You can never supply enough information to your top team for them to be informed and make a sensible decision and pass it down. The hierarchy is broken. It doesn't work. We need a networked system.

Technology is changing how decisions get made.

And it's shaping a workplace where everyone expects a unique experience: a choice of channels and personalized settings. Think back to how hard Jay Baer works to start conversations across every conceivable channel and using a variety of formats. Everyone gets a consistent message, packaged up and delivered in a way he hopes they'll like best. Jay knows people gravitate towards technologies they prefer. Ask Vic Alejandro, senior technical project manager at Denver Water. Vic is a seasoned and wry observer of tech life — and you'll also find him on the city's comedy circuit. "The bar has moved for what a good experience is," he says. "In the past, a good experience was a green-screen computer. One color. No animation. That's all you got, and you didn't complain because you didn't know any better. Now, there are so many options that people grouse at you when a font isn't the exact shade of 'burnt sienna' they saw in a graphics class they took in a neighbor's basement last summer. These are first-world problems, I guess."

The leadership lesson is simple. Your people will expect work to be collaborative, flexible, and meaningful. They also increasingly expect work to be something they log into rather than walk into.

THE CULTURE OF THE WORKPLACE: THEN AND NOW

If all of this is a surprise, where have you been hiding? The differences between millennials and their predecessors have been talked about since 1991, when historians Neil Howe and William Strauss first coined the generation's name.[73] In 2016, millennials overtook Generation X (born 1965 to 1980) as the largest single generation in the US labor force — representing about 35 percent of workers.[74] And the global food corporation Kraft Heinz made headlines in September 2017 when it appointed twenty-nine-year-old David Knopf as chief financial officer (CFO). Knopf was hailed as the first millennial on the board of a Fortune 500 company, where the average age of a CFO is fifty-two — either the first of the Generation X-ers, or the last of the baby boomer generation.[75] If your organization has a rigid management hierarchy and top-down decision-making is the normal course of business, you're already behind the cultural curve. Below is a sketch of some of the key cultural characteristics of the workplace — then and now:

20th Century Culture	21st Century Culture
Hierarchical	Egalitarian
Top-down decisions, highest-paid opinion wins	Best idea wins, whoever suggests it
Brand Matters	Ethics Matter
Working for a big-name brand matters	Working for an ethical business matters
Office-bound	Flexible
Chained to a desk; working more than 9-5	Anytime, anywhere to meet deadlines
Get ahead	Just-in-time
Sweat to deliver work early, heavy prep	Barely accomplish tasks, minimal prep
Any working tech will do	Usability matters
If this tech works, it's good enough	Does this tech feel easy to use?
Closed comms	Networked comms
Diarized communication: calls and meetings	Always available, multi-channel

Maybe you've heard of the legend of King Canute: a Viking monarch who moved his throne to the shoreline to show his courtiers that even a king didn't have the power to turn back the tide. Predictably, he got wet feet.[76] As a leader, you can try to resist the forces pushing your organization to change. Or you can adopt a leadership style that reflects a generational preference for a more open and egalitarian business culture. It's not only the tone of your leadership, but your practical decisions that will make the difference. For example, some of the cultural attributes of a modern workplace play out in employment terms and conditions, such as flexible working. James Veall predicts a future when employees will choose to take or forgo benefits from a buffet of options. They may trade salary for days off or days off for bigger pension contributions. "The days of making blanket decisions for a workforce are decreasing rapidly," says James. "Every employee has their own story. Every employee has their own set of needs." Other cultural differences relate to financial decisions leaders can make: the technology that's deployed or the company's decisions around ethical investments.

As a leader, you can try to make your people fit the business culture — or the business culture and practice better fit your people. Hint: don't get wet feet.

ARTIFICIAL INTELLIGENCE WILL NOT REPLACE HUMAN CREATIVITY

Imagine a workplace where meetings and work schedules shift in line with your monitored biorhythms to optimize your performance. Or how about neural interfaces where you think a task to completion without putting a single finger to keyboard or speaking a single voice command? The future of work is often imagined on a spectrum between the tech optimism of *Star Trek* and the grimy dystopia of *Blade Runner*.

But let's leave that to the science fiction writers. Sure, artificial intelligence and machine learning is developing at a rapid pace. Some tech firms are in such a rush to make this future *appear* to happen, they're pulling a Wizard of Oz-style trick: using the cheapest human labor they can find to pose as AI assistants to process basic emails or diary requests.[77] But the real question facing future leaders is how people and their AI-driven assistants — their "cobots" — will interact.

"I've become a real believer that we shouldn't be worried about robots taking our jobs," says James Wallman, a futurist and author whose thoughts you'll find in the *New York Times*, *Wall Street Journal*, the *Times of London* and even the likes of *GQ* and *Vice*.[78] "What we should be looking forward to is cobots coming along and supporting us."

As a leader, you're going to have to make practical decisions about what tasks are for the cobots, what tasks are for humans. Machines will always "skew tactical, humans will be strategic."[79] I'm convinced that creativity and ingenuity will be the primary human attributes of the future.

That's what this book is all about. Machines, if you pardon the pun, are bit part players in our story. Mastering modern work is about leading people. That's true today and will be true tomorrow, whatever technology enriches the workplace. Leadership is about human interaction and, at its most noble, helping people to achieve the extraordinary. The need for leaders to get the best from their teams isn't going out of fashion any time soon. I hope when Jen Gilligan and the brightest talents of her generation read this book, they'll choose to walk in step with their teams as they journey towards extraordinary goals. I hope they'll leave blame by the wayside, follow trail markers, and celebrate success along the route.

And, reader, if there's only one chapter you return to, I hope you choose the first. Making work matter is one of the greatest gifts you can give to another human. As former US president Bill Clinton once said, "Work is about more than making a living, it's fundamental to human dignity, to our sense of self-worth as useful, independent, free people." Whatever goal is set, however brilliantly conceived your plan to achieve it, you won't have mastered modern work if you haven't made it matter to people. All things considered, making work matter is the single most effective way to help people get stuff done right.

I'll end where I began, with President Kennedy's moon-shot speech in 1962. The goal he set that day was truly extraordinary: to leave the earth and set foot on an astronomical body that had bewildered and beguiled people throughout human history. "That goal," the president said, "will serve to organize and measure the best of our energies and skills, because that challenge is one that we are willing to accept, one we are unwilling to postpone, and one which we intend to win." And they did.[80]

Done Right Value Pyramid

Bring it all together to get work done—and done right

Mastering 21st century work is all about leading people toward a common vision—a grand vision that is hopeful, clearly communicated, attainable and, above all, extraordinary. Each of the exercises you've completed in this book, from crafting your commander's intent to identifying work performance indicators, has provided one small step toward making that happen. Here's a visual representation of how all the pieces fit together.

DONE RIGHT VALUE PYRAMID

A few points to note:

- Notice how those you serve (shareholders, customers and employees) are the foundation upon which you build every action and decision.

- At the top of the pyramid is your vision. All actions you take should point unfailingly toward this organizational belief.

- Your vision is supported by your commander's intent and your compass-point question, which keep all eyes trained upward.

- Your key initiatives are defined by extraordinary goals and are built from milestones, which are achieved by the relentless accomplishment of best next actions.

- Along the right side, the work performance indicators (WPIs) help you determine whether your work is moving in the right direction—and how quickly. When all arrows point upward, your efforts are paying off. Downward arrows create drag that will hold you back from making your vision a reality.

YOUR TURN

Distribute copies of the blank pyramid below to the different members of your team, and fill one out yourself. Can each person accurately state the organizational vision? Do they know the key initiatives, extraordinary goals, milestones, and best next actions that they need to accomplish in their own unique and specific roles?

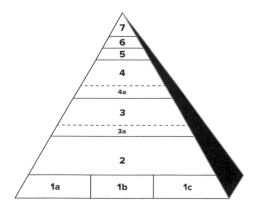

1a. Shareholders

_____
_____
_____

1b. Customers

_____
_____
_____

1c. Employees

_____
_____
_____

2. Best Next Actions

_____
_____
_____

3. Milestones

_____
_____
_____

3a. Go / No-Go Criteria

_____
_____
_____

4. Milestones

_____
_____
_____

4a. (Extraordinary Goals / Measurable Outcomes)

_____
_____
_____

5. Compass-Point Question

_____
_____
_____

6. Commander's Intent

_____
_____
_____

7. Vision

_____
_____
_____

Once everyone you lead is able to understand and accurately complete a value pyramid like this one, you'll have incontrovertible proof that every member of your team both knows their role and believes it's important. You will have made work _matter_, at all levels of the organization, which is how tomorrow's leaders will be able to make sure modern work not only gets done—but that it gets _done right_.

Appendix I:
Glossary of Terms

Best next action: The single thing you should do within the next two weeks to get closer to a milestone.

Commander's intent: A statement that clarifies the purpose of a project and articulates the end goal. It consists of outcomes, key activities, and operating constraints.

Compass-point question: One simple question that will always keep you on track and lead you back to your extraordinary goal.

Escape velocity: Occurs when milestones are being met or exceeded and progress towards completion is on track or ahead of schedule within the resources allocated to the project.

Extraordinary goal: A goal at the edge of your headlights, one that will require you to *change the way you are working today.*

Go/no-go criteria: Hard and fast rules that anyone in a leadership role can use to make the call to continue or abort the mission.

Milestone: Trail markers of progress that show how far you're moving towards completion of each key initiative.

Key initiative: Projects or actions that take an organization closer to its goals. These might be intended to improve the operational efficiency of the business, fuel innovation, address challenges from competitors, or adapt to changing market conditions.

Service statement: A statement that outlines what shareholders, employees, and customers will say when you accomplish your work.

Vision statement: A statement that gives your team a clear and compelling answer to the question *"Why am I working here?"* It's rooted in authenticity, points beyond the leader, is extraordinary but attainable, and can be easily communicated.

Work performance indicators: Five essential measurements, consisting of the mix of running vs. changing your organization, the total capacity available to get work done, the velocity of your team, the quality of work, and the amount of team engagement.

Appendix II: Charities

Workfront partners with two charities we feel passionate about supporting.

UTAH YOUTH VILLAGE

Utah Youth Village changes the lives of troubled children. Some have been abused and neglected. Others suffer from mental and emotional issues. All are lost and need super-parents. Utah Youth Village provides super-parents for the most troubled children in Utah.

Our Families First program teaches their parents how to be the super-parents they need. Some experience a very difficult time when they become teenagers.

Alpine Academy, our therapeutic boarding school for teenage girls, provides an education and specialized therapy so girls can return to their families and reclaim their lives. Some are too troubled to attend public school.

Our Youth Village Academy educates teenage boys and girls while teaching them behavioral skills so they can return to public school and work towards graduation. Some are refugees from war-torn and dangerous countries. We provide specialized proctor families for refugee children so they can assimilate and become productive citizens. Some are in loving homes and their parents want to be super-parents.

Our Smarter Parenting website and in-person classes give ALL parents the tools they need to raise happy, responsible, and ethical children.

Read more at http://www.youthvillage.org.

ONE REFUGEE

One Refugee helps refugees to enter the workforce by assisting them in earning a college degree. One Refugee provides résumé review, tutoring, and other services to make the transition to the workforce easier.

The Online Mentor Program helps people who are not local to Salt Lake to provide one-on-one assistance to refugees.

The Tutoring Program matches tutors in almost any subject with students.

Hear their stories at http://onerefugee.org.

Endnotes

1. NASA Space Movies Cinema. John F. Kennedy Moon Speech — Rice Stadium. 12 September 1962. Accessed 23 August 2018. https://er.jsc.nasa.gov/seh/ricetalk.htm. https://er.jsc.nasa.gov/seh/ricetalk.htm.

2. TEDxTalks. 2011. "TEDxAtlanta - Teresa Amabile - The Progress Principle TED Talk. https://www.youtube.com/watch?v=XD6N8bsjOEE." YouTube. October 12, 2011. https://www.youtube.com/watch?v=XD6N8bsjOEE.

3. "National Science Foundation - Where Discoveries Begin." n.d. What's Killing Trees during Droughts? Scientists Have New Answers. I NSF - National Science Foundation. Accessed September 21, 2018. https://www.nsf.gov/statistics/2018/nsf18306//.

4. Smart Insights. Dave Chaffey. "Forecast growth in percentage of online retail/"Ecommerce sales." 7 May Growth Statistics - UK, US and Worldwide Forecasts." 2018. Accessed 23 AugustMay 7, 2018. https://www.smartinsights.com/digital-marketing-strategy/online-retail-sales-growth//.

5. https://www.amazon.com/Pride-Matters-More-Than-Money/dp/0609610651 "Why Pride Matters More Than Money: The Power of the World's Greatest Motivational Force." n.d. Amazon. Accessed September 21, 2018. https://www.amazon.com/Pride-Matters-More-Than-Money/dp/0609610651.

6. WiredMason, Betsy. 2018. "The Incredible Things NASA didDid to trainTrain Apollo astronauts." Betsy Mason. 20 July 2011. Accessed 23 August 2018. https://www.wired.com/2011/07/moon-landing-gallery/

Astronauts." Wired. Conde Nast. June 7, 2018. https://www.wired.com/2011/07/moon-landing-gallery/.

7.   "The Zappos Insights Team." n.d. Zappos Insights. Accessed September 21, 2018. https://www.zapposinsights.com/about/who-we-are, https://buffer.com/about. "About Us - Buffer." n.d. The Ideal Time and Frequency to Post to Social Media [Day 4]. Accessed September 21, 2018. https://buffer.com/about.

8.   https://www.ted.com/talks/simon_sinek_how_great_leaders_inspire_action Sinek, Simon. n.d. "How Great Leaders Inspire Action." TED: Ideas Worth Spreading. Accessed September 21, 2018. https://www.ted.com/talks/simon_sinek_how_great_leaders_inspire_action.

9.   https://resources.workfront.com/project-management-blog/how-email-meetings-automation-are-shaping-the-future-of-work-2017-2018-state-of-enterprise-report-u-s-edition "How Email, Meetings, and Automation Are Shaping the Future of Work." n.d. Workfront. Accessed September 21, 2018. https://resources.workfront.com/project-management-blog/how-email-meetings-automation-are-shaping-the-future-of-work-2017-2018-state-of-enterprise-report-u-s-edition.

10. https://resources.workfront.com/project-management-blog/10-reasons-you-need-an-operational-system-of-record "10 Reasons You Need an Operational System of Record." n.d. Workfront. Accessed September 21, 2018. https://resources.workfront.com/project-management-blog/10-reasons-you-need-an-operational-system-of-record.

11. "Proverbs Chapter 29 KJV (King James Version)." n.d. King James Bible Online. Accessed September 21, 2018. https://www.kingjamesbibleonline.org/Proverbs-Chapter-29/.

12. Schurenberg, Eric. 1899. "Richard Branson: Why Customers Come Second at Virgin." Inc.com. November 30, 1899. https://www.inc.com/eric-schurenberg/sir-richard-branson-put-your-staff-first-customers-second-and-shareholders-third.html.

13. "Jack Ma - Why Customer Comes First." 2017. YouTube. October 1,

2017. https://www.youtube.com/watch?v=ZLtvBgXUp6Q.

14. Rhodes, J., Swafford, K. and Warner, J. (2017). "Dive Into the Best Letters to Shareholders." Accessed September 21, 2018. http://nacd.cms-plus.com/files/Magazine/pdf/NACD%20Directorship%20JulAug17%20Cover%20Story.pdf

15. https://www.investopedia.com/articles/basics/08/corporate-priorities.asp Beattie, Andrew. 2008. "Whom Should Corporations Please?" Investopedia. September 3, 2008. https://www.investopedia.com/articles/basics/08/corporate-priorities.asp.

16. Dräger, S. (n.d.). *DRÄGER PUBLICATIONS Company Principles.* https://www.draeger.com/Corporate/Content/company_principles.pdf

17. "What Is Servant Leadership?" n.d. Greenleaf Center for Servant Leadership. Accessed September 21, 2018. https://www.greenleaf.org/what-is-servant-leadership/.

18. https://www.youtube.com/watch?v=4BvwpjaGZCQ"How to Use a Raw Egg to Determine If Your Mattress Is Awful - Purple Mattress." 2016. YouTube. April 26, 2016. https://www.youtube.com/watch?v=4BvwpjaGZCQ.

19. Joni, Saj-nicole A., and Damon Beyer. 2010. The Right Fight, How Great Leaders use Healthy Conflict to Driver: *Six Principles for Creating Breakthrough Performance, Innovation, and Value*, Saj-Nicole Joni and Damon Beyer,. New York: Harper Business, 2010..

20. https://hbr.org/2009/07/shareholders-first-not-so-fast Pfeffer, Jeffrey. 2014. "Shareholders First? Not So Fast ..." Harvard Business Review. August 1, 2014. https://hbr.org/2009/07/shareholders-first-not-so-fast.

21. Pressfield, Steven. 2000. "Tides of War: A Novel of Alcibiades and the Peloponnesian War" Steven Pressfield. New York: Doubleday.

22. https://www.amazon.com/How-Did-That-Happen-Accountable/dp/1591844142 Connors, Roger, and Tom Smith. 2009. *How Did That Happen?: Holding People Accountable for Results the Positive, Principled Way.* New York: Portfolio.

23. The Divided Self. (n.d.). http://www.happinesshypothesis.com/happiness-hypothesis-ch1.pdf

24. The Divided Self. (n.d.). http://www.happinesshypothesis.com/happiness-hypothesis-ch1.pdf

25. Heath, C. and Heath, D. (2010). *Switch: How To Change Things When Things Are Hard.* http://www.heathbrothers.com/download/switch-chapter1.pdf

26. https://www.trekbikes.com/us/en_US/inside_trek/heritage_global/ "Inside Trek - Heritage | Trek Bikes." n.d. Bikes - The World's Best Bikes and Cycling Gear | Trek Bikes. Accessed September 21, 2018. https://www.trekbikes.com/us/en_US/inside_trek/heritage_global/.

27. "Busy." 2017. Tony Crabbe. October 25, 2017. https://tonycrabbe.com/busy//.

28. Will, George F. 2010. "'Events, Dear Boy, Events'." Newsweek. March 14, 2010. http://www.newsweek.com/events-dear-boy-events-143481.

29. https://www.youtube.com/watch?v=VlTfbGemGcM, https://www.willitmaketheboatgofaster.com/the-book/ "Will It Make the Boat Go Faster | Ben Hunt Davis." 2014. YouTube. October 14, 2014. https://www.youtube.com/watch?v=VlTfbGemGcM, https://www.willitmaketheboatgofaster.com/the-book/.

30. Barton, Michelle A., and Kathleen M. Sutcliffe. n.d. "Learning When to Stop Momentum." MIT Sloan Management Review. Accessed September 21, 2018. https://sloanreview.mit.edu/article/learning-when-to-stop-momentum/

31. "Insights Discovery® - Our Official Flagship Product and Foundation." n.d. Insights. Accessed September 21, 2018. https://www.insights.com/products/insights-discovery//.

32. https://www.weforum.org/agenda/2015/01/the-most-revealing-big-data-quotes/ Marr, Bernard. n.d. "The Most Revealing Big Data Quotes." World Economic Forum. Accessed September 21, 2018. https://www.weforum.org/agenda/2015/01/the-most-revealing-big-data-quotes/.

33. https://www.ft.com/content/3f5cc88c-0b21-11e1-ae56-00144feabdc0 Kuper, Simon. 2011. "Let's Play Moneyball." Financial Times. November 11, 2011. https://www.ft.com/content/3f5cc88c-0b21-11e1-ae56-00144feabdc0.

34. The Deciding Factor: Big Data & Decision Making. (n.d.). https://www.capgemini.com/wp-content/uploads/2017/07/The_Deciding_Factor__Big_Data___Decision_Making.pdf

35. "Interview with General Colin Powell." n.d. Executive Recruitment & Global Management Consulting. Accessed September 21, 2018. https://www.egonzehnder.com/insight/interview-with-general-colin-powell.

36. Duckworth, Angela Lee. n.d. "Grit: The Power of Passion and Perseverance." TED: Ideas Worth Spreading. Accessed September 21, 2018. https://www.ted.com/talks/angela_lee_duckworth_grit_the_power_of_passion_and_perseverance.

37. https://resources.workfront.com/ebooks-whitepapers/2017-2018-state-of-enterprise-work-report-u-s-edition 2017-2018 State of Enterprise Work Report." n.d. Workfront. Accessed September 21, 2018. https://resources.workfront.com/ebooks-whitepapers/2017-2018-state-of-enterprise-work-report-u-s-edition.

38. Connors, Roger., and Tom Smith. 2009. How Did That Happen??: Holding People Accountable for Results the Positive, Principled Way (Kindle Locations 238-245). Penguin Publishing Group. Kindle Edition. New York: Portfolio.

39. "The Differentiated Leader -: Specific Strategies for Handling Today's Adverse Situations" - Organizational Dynamics, Vol. 33, No. 3, pp 292-306, 2004).." EBSCO Online Library Search Engine Directory - Find Articles, News, Periodicals and Other Premium Online Content. Accessed September 20, 2018. http://connection.ebscohost.com/c/articles/14533098/differentiated-leader-specific-strategies-handling-todays-adverse-situations.

40. https://www.nature.com/articles/srep17390#abstract Ngo, Lawrence,

Meagan Kelly, Christopher G. Coutlee, R. McKell Carter, Walter Sinnott-Armstrong, and Scott A. Huettel. 2015. "Two Distinct Moral Mechanisms for Ascribing and Denying Intentionality." Nature News. Nature Publishing Group. December 4, 2015. https://www.nature.com/articles/srep17390#abstract.

41. http://news.bbc.co.uk/1/hi/sci/tech/452579.stm "Sci/Tech | Satellite Closes in on Mars." 1999. BBC News. BBC. September 23, 1999. http://news.bbc.co.uk/1/hi/sci/tech/452579.stm.

42. Grossman, Lisa. 2018. "Nov. 10, 1999: Metric Math Mistake Muffed Mars Meteorology Mission." Wired. Conde Nast. January 14, 2018. https://www.wired.com/2010/11/1110mars-climate-observer-report/.

43. https://hbr.org/2009/11/new-study-how-communication-dr Baldoni, John. 2014. "New Study: How Communication Drives Performance." Harvard Business Review. July 23, 2014. https://hbr.org/2009/11/new-study-how-communication-dr.

44. https://www.fastcompany.com/3051417/why-its-so-hard-to-pay-attention-explained-by-science Bellis, Rich. 2015. "Why It's So Hard To Pay Attention, Explained By Science." Fast Company. September 25, 2015. https://www.fastcompany.com/3051417/why-its-so-hard-to-pay-attention-explained-by-science.

45. https://resources.workfront.com/ebooks-whitepapers/2017-2018-state-of-enterprise-work-report-u-s-edition "2017-2018 State of Enterprise Work Report." n.d. Workfront. Accessed September 21, 2018. https://resources.workfront.com/ebooks-whitepapers/2017-2018-state-of-enterprise-work-report-u-s-edition.

46. https://www.researchgate.net/publication/305882368_Suspicion_in_the_workplace_Organizational_conspiracy_theories_and_work-related_outcomes Douglas, K. M., & Leite, A. C. (n.d.). Suspicion in the workplace: Organizational conspiracy theories and work-related outcomes. https://www.researchgate.net/publication/305882368_Suspicion_in_the_workplace_Organizational_conspiracy_theories_and_

work-related_outcomes

47. "About Us." n.d. Markempa. Accessed September 21, 2018. https://www.markempa.com/about-us/.

48. Weisberg, Jessica. 2018. "What Dale Carnegie's 'How to Win Friends and Influence People' Can Teach the Modern Worker." The New Yorker. April 4, 2018. https://www.newyorker.com/books/page-turner/what-dale-carnegies-how-to-win-friends-and-influence-people-can-teach-the-modern-worker.

49. Net promoter score is a customer loyalty metric developed and trademarked by Fred Reichheld, Bain & Company, and Satmetrix "Net Promoter." 2018. Wikipedia. Wikimedia Foundation. July 16, 2018. https://en.wikipedia.org/wiki/Net_Promoter.

50. https://www.brainyquote.com/quotes/john_wooden_386958

51. "John Wooden Quotes." n.d. BrainyQuote. Xplore. Accessed September 21, 2018. https://www.brainyquote.com/quotes/john_wooden_386958.

52. https://www.trekbikes.com/gb/en_US/equipment/cycling-accessories/bike-lights/bike-rear-lights/bontrager-flare-r-rear-bike-light/p/13202/ "Repair Time!" n.d. Bikes - The World's Best Bikes and Cycling Gear | Trek Bikes. Accessed September 21, 2018. https://www.trekbikes.com/gb/en_US/equipment/cycling-accessories/bike-lights/bike-rear-lights/bontrager-flare-r-rear-bike-light/p/13202/.

53. http://mentalfloss.com/article/63341/frederick-winslow-taylor-patron-saint-shovel "Frederick Winslow Taylor, the Patron Saint of the Shovel." 2015. Mental Floss. April 27, 2015. http://mentalfloss.com/article/63341/frederick-winslow-taylor-patron-saint-shovel.

54. "Frederick Winslow Taylor." 2009. The Economist. The Economist Newspaper. February 6, 2009. https://www.economist.com/node/13051591.

55. https://archive.nytimes.com/www.nytimes.com/books/97/06/15/reviews/970615.15willmt.html "A Faster Mousetrap Review." The New

York Times. Accessed September 21, 2018. https://archive.nytimes.com/ www.nytimes.com/books/97/06/15/reviews/970615.15willmt.html.

56. https://www.economist.com/news/2009/02/09/scientific-management"Scientific Management." 2009. The Economist. The Economist Newspaper. February 9, 2009. https://www.economist.com/ news/2009/02/09/scientific-management.

57. http://quantifiedself.com/ "Quantified Self - Self Knowledge Through Numbers." n.d. Quantified Self Guide - SenseWear. Accessed September 21, 2018. http://quantifiedself.com/.

58. http://uk.businessinsider.com/best-selling-cars-and-trucks-in-us-2017-2018-1?r=US&IR=T/#3-ram-500723-23-18 Thompson, Cadie. 2018. "The 20 Best-Selling Cars and Trucks in America." Business Insider. January 20, 2018. http://uk.businessinsider.com/best-selling-cars-and-trucks-in-us-2017-2018-1?r=US&IR=T/#3-ram-500723-23-18.

59. http://www.macrotrends.net/2585/capacity-utilization-rate-historical-chart "Capacity Utilization Rate - 50 Year Historical Chart." n.d. MacroTrends. Accessed September 21, 2018. http://www.macrotrends.net/2585/capacity-utilization-rate-historical-chart.

60. https://www.mckinsey.com/industries/high-tech/our-insights/the-social-economy https://resources.workfront.com/project-management-blog/ how-email-meetings-automation-are-shaping-the-future-of-work-2017-2018-state-of-enterprise-report-u-s-edition Chui, Michael, James Manyika, Jacques Bughin, Richard Dobbs, Charles Roxburgh, Hugo Sarrazin, Geoffrey Sands, and Magdalena Westergren. n.d. "The Social Economy: Unlocking Value and Productivity through Social Technologies." McKinsey & Company. Accessed September 21, 2018. https://www.mckinsey.com/industries/high-tech/our-insights/the-social-economy.
"How Email, Meetings, and Automation Are Shaping the Future of Work." n.d. Workfront. Accessed September 21, 2018. https://resources.workfront.com/project-management-blog/how-email-meetings-automation-are-shaping-the-future-of-work-2017-2018-state-of-

enterprise-report-u-s-edition.

61. https://blog.kissmetrics.com/loading-time/ "How Loading Time Affects Your Bottom Line." 2018. Neil Patel. July 12, 2018. https://blog. kissmetrics.com/loading-time/.

62. https://www.nytimes.com/2000/05/07/magazine/the-way-we-live-now-5-7-00-questions-for-antonio-damasio-what-feelings-feel-like.html Star, Alexander. 2000. "The Way We Live Now: 5-7-00: Questions for: Antonio Damasio; What Feelings Feel Like." The New York Times. May 7, 2000. https://www.nytimes.com/2000/05/07/magazine/the-way-we-live-now-5-7-00-questions-for-antonio-damasio-what-feelings-feel-like. html.

63. https://www.glassdoor.co.uk/Interview/How-many-ways-can-you-think-of-to-find-a-needle-in-a-haystack-How-many-haircuts-do-you-think-happen-in-America-every-year-QTN_669099.htm and https://www.inc.com/business-insider/google-hardest-interview-questions.html
"Google Interview Question: How Many Ways Can You Think o..." n.d. Glassdoor. Accessed September 21, 2018. https://www.glassdoor. co.uk/Interview/How-many-ways-can-you-think-of-to-find-a-needle-in-a-haystack-How-many-haircuts-do-you-think-happen-in-America-every-year-QTN_669099.htm. and
Kosoff, Maya. 2016. "41 Of Google's Toughest Interview Questions." Inc.com. Inc. January 21, 2016. https://www.inc.com/business-insider/google-hardest-interview-questions.html.

64. http://uk.businessinsider.com/microsoft-interview-questions-2015-10/#tell-me-how-you-would-design-an-airport-program-manager-candidate-13 Kosoff, Maya. 2015. "25 Tricky Microsoft Interview Questions You Don't Want to Be Asked." Business Insider. October 12, 2015. http://uk.businessinsider.com/microsoft-interview-questions-2015-10/#tell-me-how-you-would-design-an-airport-program-manager-candidate-13.

65. https://hbr.org/2013/03/measuring-creativity-we-have-t

Reinartz, Werner. 2014. "Measuring Creativity: We Have the Technology." Harvard Business Review. August 7, 2014. https://hbr.org/2013/03/measuring-creativity-we-have-t.

66. Martin, James R. n.d. "Roberts, M. W. and K. J. Silvester. 1996. Why ABC Failed and How It May Yet Succeed. Journal of Cost Management (Winter): 23-35." CVP Analysis and TOC. Accessed September 21, 2018. http://maaw.info/ArticleSummaries/ArtSumRoberts96.htm.

67. Fry, Richard, Ruth Igielnik, and Eileen Patten. 2018. "How Millennials Today Compare with Their Grandparents 50 Years Ago." Pew Research Center. Pew Research Center. March 16, 2018. http://www.pewresearch.org/fact-tank/2018/03/16/how-millennials-compare-with-their-grandparents/.

68. "For Digital Nomads, Work Is Where the Laptop Is." 2018. The Washington Post. WP Company. July 6, 2018. https://www.washingtonpost.com/business/economy/for-digital-nomads-work-is-where-the-laptop-is/2018/07/06/3e146a4c-7e34-11e8-bb6b-c1cb691f1402_story.html?noredirect=on&utm_term=.27991ab07c59.

69. http://www.pewresearch.org/fact-tank/2018/03/16/how-millennials-compare-with-their-grandparents/; http://www.pewresearch.org/fact-tank/2018/05/02/millennials-stand-out-for-their-technology-use-but-older-generations-also-embrace-digital-life/
Jiang, Jingjing. 2018. "Millennials Stand out for Their Technology Use." Pew Research Center. May 2, 2018. http://www.pewresearch.org/fact-tank/2018/03/16/how-millennials-compare-with-their-grandparents/; http://www.pewresearch.org/fact-tank/2018/05/02/millennials-stand-out-for-their-technology-use-but-older-generations-also-embrace-digital-life/.

70. 41 percent of US citizens aged 65 or older use Facebook. Smith, Aaron, and Monica Anderson. 2018. "Appendix A: Detailed Table I Pew Research Center." Pew Research Center: Internet, Science & Tech. March 1, 2018. http://www.pewinternet.org/2018/03/01/social-media-use-2018-appendix-a-detailed-table/.

71. https://thenextweb.com/insider/2011/08/06/20-years-ago-today-the-world-wide-web-opened-to-the-public/ Bryant, Martin. 2016. "20 Years Ago Today, the World Wide Web Was Born - TNW Insider." The Next Web. March 3, 2016. https://thenextweb.com/insider/2011/08/06/20-years-ago-today-the-world-wide-web-opened-to-the-public/.

72. https://www.forbes.com/sites/samanthasharf/2015/08/24/what-is-a-millennial-anyway-meet-the-man-who-coined-the-phrase/#2aac55894a05
Sharf, Samantha. 2016. "What Is A 'Millennial' Anyway? Meet The Man Who Coined The Phrase." Forbes. Forbes Magazine. September 6, 2016. https://www.forbes.com/sites/samanthasharf/2015/08/24/what-is-a-millennial-anyway-meet-the-man-who-coined-the-phrase/#2aac55894a05.

73. Fry, Richard. 2018. "Millennials Are Largest Generation in the U.S. Labor Force." Pew Research Center. April 11, 2018. http://www.pewresearch.org/fact-tank/2018/04/11/millennials-largest-generation-us-labor-force/.

74. https://www.washingtonpost.com/news/on-leadership/wp/2017/09/11/a-29-year-old-is-the-new-cfo-of-the-company-behind-jell-o-and-oscar-meyer-weiners/?utm_term=.52562094b35d
"A 29-Year-Old Is the New CFO of the Company behind Jell-O and Oscar Mayer Weiners." 2017. The Washington Post. WP Company. September 11, 2017. https://www.washingtonpost.com/news/on-leadership/wp/2017/09/11/a-29-year-old-is-the-new-cfo-of-the-company-behind-jell-o-and-oscar-meyer-weiners/?utm_term=.52562094b35d.

75. Sometimes, the legend gets told the other way around … that Canute tried to show his power rather than its limits. But either way, the point holds true: leaders can't hold back the tide.
"Canute (Knud) The Great." n.d. A Viking Raid. Accessed September 21, 2018. http://www.viking.no/the-viking-kings-and-earls/canute-knud-the-great/.

76. https://www.theguardian.com/technology/2018/jul/06/artificial-

intelligence-ai-humans-bots-tech-companies?
Solon, Olivia. 2018. "The Rise of 'Pseudo-AI': How Tech Firms Quietly Use Humans to Do Bots' Work." The Guardian. Guardian News and Media. July 6, 2018. https://www.theguardian.com/technology/2018/jul/06/artificial-intelligence-ai-humans-bots-tech-companies.

77. "James Wallman." n.d. James Wallman. Accessed September 21, 2018. https://jameswallman.wordpress.com/.

78. Pistrui, Joseph. 2018. "The Future of Human Work Is Imagination, Creativity, and Strategy." Harvard Business Review. January 18, 2018. https://hbr.org/2018/01/the-future-of-human-work-is-imagination-creativity-and-strategy.

79. https://er.jsc.nasa.gov/seh/ricetalk.htm "John F. Kennedy Moon Speech - Rice Stadium." NASA. Accessed September 21, 2018. https://er.jsc.nasa.gov/seh/ricetalk.htm.

Acknowledgments

It all starts with Art Wilson. I have lost count of the nights I spent with Art at his ranch, Fabra-Acres, outside of Boerne, Texas. Art is my mentor and thirty years ago introduced me to the concept of the *best next action*. I get things done today because Art showed me the way.

Done Right does not exist without Paul Hill: sensei, muse, and writer extraordinaire. Paul spent countless hours late at night from his home base in the UK collaborating on the manuscript. He was always of great humor and had amazing insights, wide-ranging curiosity, and great patience with me. And most important, I got to relive childbirth vicariously through Sabelline and Paul as they brought beautiful little Célestine Marie into the world during our project.

Angie Lucas did an amazing job of being second eyes, ears, and brain and was awesome at developing the exercises at the end of each chapter.

The nudge machine in the trifecta of Heather Hurst, Shelbi Gomez, and Jon Ogden were relentless in making sure this book was Done Right Now.

Paige Hoyt allowed me to have a special relationship with time, getting Paul and me together amongst everything else going on.

Finally, I'd like to acknowledge the more than 1,000 Workfront teammates who each day live out our values of Doing Great Work, Finishing Strong, Obsessing Over Customers, and Winning Together.

Implement with Workfront

Want to implement the principles and practices in this book across your company so you can face the digital crisis head on?

Look no further than Workfront.

We've helped thousands of companies successfully transform their businesses into modern enterprises that increase revenue, improve customer experiences, and eliminate cost. Above all, Workfront gives you the power to automate and enable the principles in this book.

- Consolidated features all in one easy-to-use tool
- Centralized feedback and approvals accessible to the entire team
- Standardized templates to save time and improve accuracy

See more at Workfront.com.

About the Author

Alex Shootman, president and CEO at Workfront, is fortunate to have more than twenty-five years of leadership experience at technology companies ranging from IBM, BMC Software, and Vignette, to modern SaaS-based companies like Apptio and Eloqua. Along the way he established a reputation for "Getting it Done" and "Doing it Right" in high-pressure situations. He is married to his college sweetheart, Brettne, who still laughs at his bad jokes after thirty-four years and celebrates when his clothing is back in style every eight years. Together they have four great kids, Will, Sam, Remy, and Tara. In his free time, Alex can be found trying to convince his legs that they really don't hurt on a road bike, admiring the view from a 14er in Colorado, or breathing bubbles down on a reef in his home state of Hawaii. Follow him on Twitter at @Shootman.